16/6/95

A very happy 'advanced'
b'day to Numi Apa
from
Safi & Anju

A HEART FULL OF
BURDEN

In India, what passes for democracy is not democracy. It does not have any of the elements of democracy. There is no will of the people. There is no rule by consent. There is no administration of justice... the country is seeing a loss of faith in that which passes for democracy. All of us are collectively responsible for the tragic pass to which we have brought this country.

———— ☆ ————

There is a law in this country for every purpose...the per capita availability of laws in the world is nowhere as high as in India. And implementation of them is nowhere as deficient as in India.

———— ☆ ————

I went to Kashmir in 1989 to find out what was happening. When I came back I wrote a report where I said if I were a Kashmiri I would have indulged in greater violence.

———— ☆ ————

Since the last four years I have been searching for one square foot of this country which is made up of dry sand. I am not talking of Rajasthan desert. I am looking for dryness which is not impregnated with corruption.

———— ☆ ————

Today, with no disrespect to anybody, there are leaders, but there are no leaders who are Titans. Most of our leaders today, I regret to say, are pygmies.

———— ☆ ————

There is one-half of the population which is oppressed, depressed, suppressed, compressed. They are called women. There are parts of India where the literacy rate of women, today, is as low as three per cent.

———— ☆ ————

In all the cities of this country there is no power shedding because power shedding does not take place in India. There is load shedding. Nobody sheds power. It is a characteristic of power that once you acquire it, either by election or by appointment, you never shed it.

T. N. Seshan

A HEART FULL OF BURDEN

UBSPD

UBS Publishers' Distributors Ltd.
5 Ansari Road, New Delhi-110 002
Bombay Bangalore Madras Calcutta Patna Kanpur London

First Published 1995

ISBN 81-7476-027-X

Cover design: **UBS Art Studio**
Cover photo: **Nitin Rai/Sunday**

Designed & Typeset at UBSPD in 11 pt. Souvenir
Printed at Rajkamal Electric Press, Delhi

To
My Mother

Contents

Introduction — 9

1. "That Which is Called India" — 15

2. Are We Cockroaches? — 37

3. A Conspiracy of Silence — 50

4. When Knowledge Outstrips Wisdom — 76

5. "Rishvateva Jayate" — 95

6. History is Good for Lunch, Not for Sleep — 114

7. University of the World — 135

8. 'The Rich Get Richer, the Poor Get Children' — 141

Index — 153

Introduction

A little more than 44 years ago, on 26 November 1949, we, the People of India, adopted, enacted and gave unto ourselves our Constitution, laying down, thereby, our solemn resolve to constitute our motherland into a Sovereign Socialist Democratic Republic and to secure to all its citizens Justice, Liberty, Equality and Fraternity. While elaborating the forms of these fundamentals of our Republic we left little out of view, perhaps as a wishful flourish of the principles on which we fought the struggle for Independence; or perhaps because we were too sure that the monolithic structure of our ancient culture will be fit to support the multifaceted edifice.

Today, when the second generation of free Indians is about to hand over the reins of the country to a third, the cardinal question whether, and to what degree, we have realised our ambitious goals continues to remain unanswered. It is my considered belief that we are not leaving much hope for the next generation. Social, economic and political justice has been hogged by the privileged few. Liberty of thought, expression, faith and worship, which was supposed to widen the spiritual and intellectual horizons of the human soul, has become the most handy instrument of exploitation of human personality. Equality of status and opportunity is buried under the garbage heap of dishonesty and corruption. And fraternity, assuring the dignity of the individual and the integrity of the nation, has become a commercial exhibition reserved only for the Republic Day.

We have perhaps yet to realise that our over-ripe culture is in an advanced state of decay. What is good in it is no longer alive and has been overtaken by the destructive element of international trade winds. The metal frame that we adopted from our erstwhile rulers to sustain us through the teething times has developed grievous metal fatigue. We are at the cross-roads and have to choose the straight and narrow path if we are to achieve our ambitions.

If a statement of truth gets a man dubbed a cynic, call me so. I am not a cynic. I am not an escapist either. Nor do I deny the astronomical leaps taken by the country, particularly in comparison with those who gained freedom at the same time in history as India. We were at a starvation corner in 1947. Today we are not only self-sufficient in food but are among its exporters. And the fact that this green revolution was achieved by a totally uneducated peasantry and in a god-forsaken underdeveloped hinterland is a miracle to be seen and believed. We had a wretched skeleton of an industrial base, mainly composed of agro-products, and a small number of textile mills, coalfields and ore mines. Today we are the tenth largest industrialised nation of the world, manufacturing or at least assembling almost everything from a safety pin to a supersonic aircraft. From a nation which perforce, under an alien and self-seeking rule, produced only office clerks, we have now become a nation whose prowess as the third largest bank of techno-economic manpower is unquestioned. All this cannot be denied.

But the dignity of the individual, the inner strength of human character, and the courage to accept and do only that which a man in his conscience believes to be correct, that self-respecting mettle which is nurtured only by true education and persistent exercise, and "maketh a nation great and strong" in the true sense is as deplorable today in the age of the supersonic aircraft as it was in the age of the bullock-cart.

The India of my dreams is not an India of high-tech economic advancement. It is a vision which perhaps died with the freedom fighters — "where the mind is without fear and the head is held high" — it is that haven of freedom into which we still have to lead our ancient nation. The dignity of the individual which is at the heart of the cosmic concept of fraternity and national pride is inalienable to my dream of a strong and free India. Justice, Liberty, Equality and Fraternity — the hallmarks of a living democracy — are elusive ideals unless the individual gets his due.

A democracy is one in which the rule of law prevails. People are ruled by consent enshrined in the laws made by their chosen representatives, and have a right to dissent and challenge that which is illegal and underhand. Coercion of any kind, mental, economic, political or intellectual, is a form of violence and should find no place in any democracy. From a statistical point of view we have the largest number of laws covering and uncovering almost every aspect of human life. But the inside out of Indian democracy today is that law is obeyed more in circumvention and defiance than in effect. Consider the case of two Indian women who were raped in the Arabian deserts in 1991. The guilty were brought to book and executed in a record time of six months; and compare it with the thousands of rapes which were committed in 1991 in India and even if, out of some of these cases charges are framed, they are still under a review. Justice in such circumstances can only be called a joke.

A democracy is one in which the true choice of the people gets reflected in the public representatives. We have yet to make a beginning in that direction. Elections in India continue to yield to the manipulative tactics of the privileged few whether privileged by sheer dint of being in power at the sacred time of the poll or being privileged to be able to commandeer enough financial resources to influence and purchase the people's choice. A third category of the privileged professionals who are swarming the holy precincts of our legislatures are the musclemen who first worked for those who began to depend on them to browbeat the voters and then preferred to displace their erstwhile masters. Absence of purity in our election process is at the root of corruption in India. I dream of an India in which the voter shall be able to assert his true choice and will be free and aware enough to identify the appropriate man for the helm of affairs.

Public awareness is the key to a vibrant and living democracy — awareness of what ails the nation, what are our ills and what remedies are best under the prevailing environment, awareness of what are the rights and obligations of the citizens and what a faithful exercise of these rights will contribute towards the general good and well-being of all.

And this awareness which has always been the proud possession of the vibrant Indian psyche has played second fiddle all through our recent post-Independence period. Our system of education is still limited in its approach. "Education", said Hazlitt, "is that which remains in us after we have forgotten what we learnt in books." Education in India is still only bookish and merely career-oriented. It does not train fully grown, aware and self-assured young men and women to swim confidently in the tumultuous ocean of the competitive and conflict-ridden society. Women who constitute half the mass of people are still by and large deprived.

The India of my dreams, though technologically keeping pace with the world and economically sound and self-sustaining, will be only an India of clay and mud if the foundations are not built on human character and honesty sustained by education which nurtures the human personality in its true sense.

1

"That Which is Called India"

I have a heart full of burden that is called India. No, that is a wrong set of words. India is not a burden. I have a heart that is full of this condition of India today. Today is Gandhi Jayanti and it is a time for stock-taking.

When we won Independence, Gandhiji was somewhere in a village in Noakhali. Six months later, he had been shot dead. Between 15 August 1947, 2 October 1947, 30 January 1948, and today, what has happened in this country? If you take note of what has happened in the last 46 years and then extrapolate that as a scientist would do, between A.D. 2000 and 2020, then you can make a reasonable assumption of what the future holds for us. It is possible to say in a nutshell that what we need to do is to

---

Speech made at the annual function of Saptahik Sakal, Pune, on 2 October 1993.

go back to *Dharma*. By *Dharma*, I do not mean a *Dharma* of A religion, B religion or C religion or X sect or Y sect or Y caste or Z subcaste. *Dharma* in its ultimate reality is the true path. It is in that secular sense that I use the word *Dharma.*

On the midnight of 14-15 August 1947, Pandit Nehru spoke on the floor of Parliament, "India will awake to freedom". He said several things all of which I am not going to quote and make life difficult for you and for myself. Among many things, he said that "we are a free and sovereign people. I am the first servant of the people". Gandhiji has shown us the true principles on which to work. Always keep the suffering masses in your mind. Industry must progress, but it should not progress at the cost of increasing inequalities by the concentration of wealth in the hands of a few to the detriment of many. All of us owe a common allegiance to that which is called India.

Between 1947 and today, what has happened? Have we not progressed? From a cantonment which was the home of all retired, and people of retiring disposition, has not Pune become a bustling industrial city, where all kinds of things are made and sent to the rest of the country, and the world? Has not the rest of the country progressed? At Independence we did not know how to make a pin, but today we can make not only planes, but rockets which sometimes fall into the sea, and certainly a satellite with which five metro channels will be with you any moment. Anybody who says we have not progressed in the last 46 years is guilty of unnecessary pessimism, guilty of unnecessarily trying to weaken the minds and hearts of the younger people. And that is certainly not my intention. But between 1947 and today, I'll ask this question and I'll give you no answer, has not much of the rhetoric remained rhetoric? Why has this happened?

The world has developed in an extraordinarily dynamic fashion. Twenty years ago if somebody had said that you will see several channels on television either by cable or by dish you would have considered him *pagal*. Several other things are happening. Even India's telephones have started working. In the world, a country which was considered, if not the first, at least between the first two, is now bitterly involved in tearing itself apart through its entrails. Other parts of the world which are tearing themselves apart are from Azerbaijan to Abkhasia to Georgia to Uzbekistan, in Central Asia, to much of tormented Africa, from Somalia to Ethiopia to Namibia. In different parts of the world, different people are pulling each other's entrails out. Now, have we adjusted ourselves in this country to this dynamic atmosphere of change? I will ask that question and leave it unanswered for you to think about it.

I shall pick up a few things which Panditji said on that fateful night and say a few words which have relevance to the screen in front of which you have to judge a question about what kind of elections are we running, what type of democracy are we running. Panditji spoke of the political people who would be servants. He spoke of the industrial people, who would be servants, or at least trustees on behalf of the poor. He spoke of a civil service. He spoke of the judical service. Now, starting in 1947, we survived for a few years on the basis of mutual confidence and harmony where issues were settled sometimes with arguments, sometimes with acrimony, rarely ever with a loss of the sense of confidence or an accumulating sense of despair. But, today when someone comes and talks to me of his optimism at lunch break, I have reasons to pinch my shirt and say I dare not say anything against him. But, in the deepest recesses of my mind, I ask, is he not an eccentric? From being honest servants, every category has become self-seekers and self-servers without exception. You make a quick fix, you make a quick buck. It matters not. Gandhiji told us means are as important as ends. Today means mean nothing, ends alone matter. They spoke of our being free and sovereign. Free for whom, sovereign for whom and the answer is, there has been a steadfast and steady erosion of all the institutions and all things which go to make up for freedom. All that we built to enshrine freedom has been eroded by a plethora of decrees, laws, rules, ordinances which serve a few; it serves the State, but not the citizens. Today, it has become desperately difficult for the citizens to defend themselves against the onslaught of laws, rules and ordinances, and against the overpowering destruction of individual freedom and dignity.

The pillars of freedom which we fought for, have been weakened and we have reached a stage, as one historian said, in which there is palsy at the centre and paralysis at the periphery. We make speeches particularly on Gandhi Jayanti day of high principles. But the only height I can see is the height of the rostrum. The rest of the principles are, if I may suddenly switch to Hindi, '*Sare ko mithi men mila dia*'.

Where are our high principles? What are high principles? Where do you search for these high principles? I am not able to see many. This is because maybe I am blind. There are people less blind who may be seeing these high principles in some part or the other of this country's existence. Everywhere you look there is a leader. But there are no heroes because heroes are not based upon authority granted to them. Leadership is not a matter of authority or privilege. Leadership is a matter of living by high principles. Leadership is not achieved by the closed end of a suitcase.

How many men of these enormous high principles can you remember on 2 October or 14 November or on 5 December? The significance of 5th of December, I am sure, many of you do not know. Rajaji, Abdul Kalam Azad, Sir Tej Bahadur Sapru, Dr. Rajendra Prasad, Bhimrao Ramji Ambedkar, Alladi Sri Krishnaswami Aiyer, I can go on listing the names of those heroes. The average Indian does not merely look for a leader. He looks for a hero — and today a hero who is totally invisible because in the minds of the average Indian a hero is a hero only because he adheres to high principles.

Leadership, as I said, is not a passport to privileges, but a demand for the acceptance of responsibility. Leaders must recognise the need to impose discipline on themselves, before trying to impose discipline on others. The congruence between words on the one side and deeds on the other, between behaviour on the one side and beliefs and values on the other, is what is called personal integrity. Today you can use an electron microscope on different parts of the country and you will find exceptionally few people of personal integrity. You talk of Motilal Nehru, you talk of Panditji, you talk of Sardar Patel, you talk of Maulana Azad, you talk of Ambedkar. They were men who were Titans. Today with no disrespect to anybody there are leaders, but there are no leaders who are Titans. Most of our leaders today, I regret to say, are pygmies.

The other principle which democracy and independence wanted us to achieve for this country was the interest of the masses. What have we done for the interest of the masses during the last 46 years? We have completely reformed the educational system and arrived at an algebra which says, $11 + 2 + 2$ is fantastically different algebra from $10 + 2 + 3$. There was a Gandhiji in this country who by merely changing the name of everybody who was called *Achooth* into Harijan, the children of God, made a social sea change. There was Bhimrao Ramji Ambedkar who wrote every ounce of his wisdom into the Constitution of India. But look at today's conditions. Take education, take health, take nutrition, take drinking water, take employment and if all of these could be integratedly called the quality of life, can you stand up and say that the quality of life has improved today from that of my father and his father? True, the population of India is growing relentlessly at a rate of 2.25 to 2.75 per cent a year. What happened in other countries is happening here also, that is, the death rate dropped dramatically when we allegedly got rid of malaria, small-pox, typhoid and cholera (although some of them are coming back with a vengeance). The birth rate did not drop equally fast because to a hungry family the addition of an extra child involves sharing the same amount of food. One extra mouth need not necessarily mean getting extra food. But two extra hands are good enough to pick up cow-dung at the end of the day.

Look at the matters which contribute to improved quality of life. As I told you, you can make your own standards as to what improves the ordinary person's quality of life — education, health, nutrition, employment, housing, water. I would not dare to tell you what ought to go into the quality of life.

What we must consider is allocation of money.

The allocations made are poor and from every rupee which gets allocated, 98 paise is lost in transmission, and two paise reaches the ultimate poor. I want to mention that we are reaching a condition where the poor are no longer willing to sit down and listen to rhetorics, whether it is 2 October, or whether it is 30 January, or whether it is 19 November, or whether it is 15 August, or any other day.

They are ready to try other and less peaceful methods as means of survival which you can see across the length and breadth of the country from Kathiawar to Kamrup and from Kashmir to Kanyakumari. Even the poor quantities of funds allocated for improving the quality of life are misused as I mentioned. They do not reach the person for whom it is meant. We have practised socialistic principles for 46 years or more. At the end of it, today, 20 per cent of India's population takes 52 per cent of its gross national income and 40 per cent of the population takes 2 per cent of the national income. Now, if only that 52 per cent of the national income could be brought down to 50 and redistributed to this poor 40 per cent, what an extraordinary improvement in their quality of life would occur! This must be taken into account. I want to summarise this part of my statement by saying that all systems, human systems, and other systems follow a certain cycle of birth and existence, growth, decay, disease and death. This is not written in today's books. This is written in Adi-Shankara's treatises *Shad Bhava Manasa Jata*. But what is required on the part of a wise society is the ability to intervene at appropriate times to make sure that the changes take place in favour of the needy, the poor and the suffering as distinct from the rich and the greedy. What you need is an internal audit to find out whether the goals of the society are being achieved or not.

This system must be capable of deciding long-term policy. It must be holistic. And above all, it must be capable of being cooperatively administered because if you think that the rule to keep to the left of the road is going to be observed only by posting enough policemen, even then many people would not obey that rule.

We want to move into a true democracy — a democracy with long-term principles, a democracy which gives you freedom, which cares for the suffering, which improves their quality of life and which does not make the rich richer and the poor burdened with more children.

Without getting into the question of backward and forward classes, and I am not a votary against rectifying the sins of thousands of years of oppression and suppression which we have given to many classes of our people, I think they must be protected, they must be brought up, they must not be asked to compete in open competitions. They must have a reserved compartment or compartments for themselves. How big, how many, what percentage, these are the issues which I have neither the ability nor the intelligence nor the intention to go into.

There is one-half of the population which is oppressed, depressed, suppressed, compressed. They are called women. There are parts of India where the literacy rate of women, today, is as low as 3 per cent. Yes, there is Kerala where women's literacy is almost 100 per cent. That is why its quality of life is comparable to that of countries much more advanced. Yes, it can lead to certain arguments. I belong to Kerala, so I can criticise Kerala with a certain degree of vehemence, which otherwise would be misunderstood. But for God's sake when all this has been done, get back to a system which rewards merit and values. That is the fundamental background against which we have to judge India's democracy and its elections. If we do not do so, the fabric on which you are painting is going to get torn. The whole country will get damaged — in Manipur, in Nagaland, in Assam, in Bodoland, in Jharkhand, in Raipur, through the PWG areas of Andhra, MP and Maharashtra; through the Naxalite areas as they are called for want of any other name.

Going deep down to the South, maybe there are other areas where other kinds of weapons from other places are now in superabundance. There is an abundance of lethal weapons of special variety which are being imported into Bombay, and sent to different parts of the country. Punjab is just coming out of its long dark night of agony, and Kashmir is still in the middle of its very great agony. The largest part of this canvas of cloth which is today's India is giving way at warp and weft. You may embroider it, you may appliqué it, you may put mirror work on it, but if the cloth is not there, all this mirror work will be unwearable.

I want to ask the older generation "is it their intention to leave to the next generation of India a legacy which is distinctly poorer than what our fathers got us"? That is the fundamental question of democracy today. If that is the gloomy background that I paint, I apologise. Today, when somebody says I have optimism, I also tell him after the poet, "breathes there a man with soul so dead who never to himself has said, this is my own, my native land". I also do so. Then half-a-minute later comes before my eyes a booth in Bihar where voting starts at 7 o'clock in the morning and at 7.15, 105 per cent of the votes have been cast. I want to present this background to you. And also tell you that if you don't change by non-violent means, they will change you by violent means. Who are they? There is a saying in my mother tongue which is Malayalam: The man who is strong will not give me even if I am hungry; and the hungry will not let go. The hunger for food, the hunger for cloth, the hunger for a roof over their heads. They will take over in means less than non-violent, if you don't clean this.

Hence democracy, elections, accountability, free change, change by consent, change under the rule of law, that is the fundamental issue of democracy and elections. I've asked myself this question: Why do we need elections? What does an election do, why is an election important? So that all kinds of posters can be printed, so that, you can fit all kinds of mikes and loud-speakers, so that you can use all kinds of running and non-running vans and vehicles? And somebody's face which you have not seen for the last five years will come back and say: "Do you remember me? I came five years ago. I have come back to you for your valuable vote. Please vote for me."

An election, I venture to suggest to you, is a method which enables conflicting values to become clearer. What is more important for this country? Is it a ski rink in Gulmarg? Is it a Centaur Hotel in Gulmarg? I can suggest other examples closer home. Are these more important or is it more important that the poor and the needy should have *roti, kapda aur makān.*

If this clear enunciation of values, does not take place, then an election is a fiction. So today you can ask me the question; Is an election a fact or a fiction? *Main Yadav hoon, yeh Jat hai, yeh Marathi ha, yeh Gujarati hai, main Brahmin hoon, ye Iyanger hain.* Not many know what the difference between a *Khatri* or an *Arora* is. If that is the fundamental on which you are going to build an election, then the election is a fiction. An election is the only thing which produces checks and balances during the administration of democracy. An election is the only thing which produces accountability. An election is the only method which delineates alternative systems of policy and ideas. It evaluates performances, it enforces accountability, it exposes the evils of society. "Please vote for me because I am of so and so religion, I am of so and so caste, I am of so and so language." Somebody said if you do not speak that language, or if you do not profess this caste and religion, we will kill you and throw your body in the river. That is not an election of any kind.

In the registers which I possess in the Election Commission today, there are still six national parties, I will say in the order as they come to my mind. Don't say Seshan said this party first, therefore, he is a sympathiser of that party. BJP is there, Congress is there, CPM is there, CPI is there, Janta Dal is there, Janta Party is there. There are 42 State parties. Republician Party comes to my mind while talking of Bombay and Maharashtra. So far as I remember, there are two groups in that party. But I have nothing to do with that. Then there are DMK, AIADMK, Assam Gana Parishad, Nutan Assam Gana Parishad. I have got 42 recognised state parties and I have 400 registered but unrecognised parties.

What kind of behaviour are we getting from the political parties? When we got freedom we had a civil service. Those days everyone was proud of the Indian Administrative Service, of which I myself am an extinguished ex-participant. Today, IAS stands for saying *I Am Sorry*. But is it only the IAS which has reached this condition? No way. You look at the men in uniform. What have we reduced them to? I do not blame the constable on the beat, the subinspector at the police station, or inspector of police incharge of the circle. But I would like to comment on the bigwigs who are occupying chairs in Bombay, Delhi, Calcutta and Madras. What men are they? Are they men of steel or are they men of bamboo? I tell everybody that by the end of my tenure in the Election

Commission I will be left with absolutely no friends in the civil service. They were never my friends in any case. If you could summarise the condition of the civil services today, I do not only mean the police and the IAS, I mean people in engineering, people in medicine, people in education all over the place. I am reminded of my zoological lessons which I never learnt, which has converted these people from people who were called vertebrata into invertebrata. Whoever is in power is willing to be authoritarian and misuse it, least of which is monetary corruption. The rest of it is moral corruption. "Hah! This man must be mad. He must have made his own pot of money when he was in service." You can check my account through the CBI. Today, I would say that monetary corruption is a far less evil than moral corruption, which has set in.

Six, seven years ago, I was the Environment Secretary. Once we had to prohibit the export of frogs' legs. Someone was very keen to export a quantity of 40 tonnes of frogs' legs. You can imagine the number of frogs to be killed in order to get 40 tonnes of frogs' legs. As he was planning to export them from West Bengal, we went and captured him in Calcutta. Overnight, he shifted to Madras, so we caught him in Madras. The Minister A who was interested in the subject spoke to the Minister B who was the Minister incharge of Environment and who is one of the outstanding Chief Ministers of the country today. He said the shipment has to be sent somehow. But I said I won't allow it. The Minister still said "it has to be sent somehow. What do you know about the law". I said I know the necessary law. I sent the file to the Law Department and the Law Department agreed with me. Even then the Minister insisted that it has to be sent somehow. Because the minister did not know Hindi well, I wrote in the file in Hindi, *'Hoga hoga, bad nam hoga, lekin hoga badnam nam aap ka, agar himmat ho to file mein hukum chalaiye.'*

Why have we lost the ability to stand up and say this is right and that is wrong, this is the rule of law, that is *not* the rule of law. During the elections you see an enormous amount of information and disinformation being distributed. An election is a time at which the public at large has the ability to sift between what is information and what is disinformation. An election is the time at which intensive mass awareness is created. This leader said something, that leader said some other thing. Where is the promised road, the school, the primary health centre? And even if there is a health centre there is no doctor, no nurse, no medicine. An election, as I already said, is a non-violent means of changing the future. I venture to suggest that this country, in the last 45 years, took elections as one more *mela* to be celebrated. Pune is a place where Bal Gangadhar Tilak said "freedom is my birth right" and he was the man who made the Ganesh festival a major event. But election is not Ganapati Bappa Moriya. Elections are hard business. I am a religious man, and I dare not say anything against Vinayaka.

What has damaged our election system, you might ask. I can list several deformities and defects. I am not again stating this in order of importance lest somebody should say that "he is definitely against so and so. He is against Indira Gandhi". In this connection I would want to refer to personality cult. We have created personality cults of big personalities, medium personalities and small personalities, but the majority of them possess feet of clay. During the entire process of the life of an Assembly or Parliament, there is a breach of trust, there is defection. You can make a law today/tomorrow. But we have more capability to break the law. Twenty-one divided by three is not equal to six. To make it equal to seven we need to produce a particular bottle of whisky. We do not seem to have a presentation of a clear alternative. If you come to a four-road crossing, one road says if you take this road you will go to this direction, if you take that road, you go to that place. There are many parties in this country today of whom it is not possible to say what are they for.

We certainly have an extremely defective election system. This election system in many senses, I apologise and say, is a joke. You have a political system which is entirely hierarchical and which is built on the foundations of sand. There are not even bricks at the bottom. We all say there should be panchayati raj, panchayat samity, zila parishads. But if you go into the roots of these bodies in the villages and the blocks and districts, they are there more in name, they are there on board, not the zila board but the board in front of the office. In much of the last 45 years the real poor have never been allowed to vote. The elections are based on the victory of money power and they are based on corrupt practices. In Malayalam, they say, do you know how elections are run in this country? Liquor for the father, cloth for the mother and food for the baby.

And then, of course, there are bombs and grenades, and country-made pistols, and now everyday we are advancing technologically, from machine-guns to submachine-guns to AK 47, AK 74 and RDX which the Maharashtra people must be particularly fond of. Ultimately, the bodies which ought to be representational have become non-representational.

Accountability seems to have disappeared and the mass of the Indian electorate do not seem to know how to shake off an unacceptable representative and to bring in an acceptable representative. I do not want to commit breach of privilege of Parliament. I have other means by which I am ready to be impeached. So I do not need one more. But those who are supposed to be accountable, are they accountable? and I again quote Pontius Pilate. He asked "what is truth?" And he did not wait for an answer. Why are the elections so? Elections are so because the law is weak. The defects are structural. I can go and put my hands on my hips and say, do you know how I conduct an election? I have now 550 million or 55 crores of voters. I run the elections from

800,000 polling booths and each polling booth has a minimum of five people. Therefore, I have four million people working for the elections, besides the policemen who are something else again.

Misuse of the system is extraordinarily profitable. I should not be asked to say more because I may be hauled up for contempt of an Assembly or Parliament. But if you reach one of those coveted places, the gains are absolutely enormous. Manipulation is the order of the day. There is an abundance of misuse of office. It has spread all over the place, from the head to the heart, to the kidney to the liver, to the limbs. Why has this been so? One of the reasons is the non-participation of the many. "Why should I go to the polling booth. Today is a holiday, I will go leisurely after lunch." And by that time someone would have cast your vote. You may go and shake your fist at the polling officer and say "but I have not voted. Look at my finger, there is no mark". But he says, "Sir, you are not the voter, the voter has already come and voted" because somebody was waiting for you not to turn up.

I venture to suggest to you that if we live for a hundred years more, let us change the election law and give the voting right to only the educated. What kind of educated? You drive on the street of your town, you will see the qualitative difference between a car driver and a cycle driver, as to who is more educated. You go to a college. You are educated. Entering the portals of a college is not education. It is humility which is the sign of education. Knowledge is a sign of education. Duty is a sign of education. At times one thinks, perhaps if our educational system were not entirely what it is today, I would want to say, abolish it. But then tomorrow the *Indian Express* would carry the headline, "Seshan condemns education". But I am not afraid of headlines.

Why are elections bad? You may ask "what are you doing about it. You only come and talk about these bad things". If you opened the newspapers of yesterday, today and tomorrow, you will see what I am doing about it. I had a constituency in Tiruchirapalli, in Tamil Nadu in the last elections, where there were only 356 candidates and the ballot paper did not look like a sheet of today's newspaper, it looked like today's edition of a newspaper. Last year we had a by-election in Delhi when Lal Krishna Advani resigned his seat. I think it was fought by two *hathis*, if I use my language correctly. They were Shatrughan Sinha and Rajesh Khanna. But there were 105 names on that ballot paper and to a slightly uneducated man like me it took about five minutes to find what I wanted to find, as to whom to vote for.

Our electoral rolls too can have any number of mistakes. I was once sent to Dehra Dun as member of the ONGC to vote. It was not an entirely low-level job. The polling officer said "everything is all right, your age is correct, your name is right. But against your name it is mentioned *female*. So how can you vote?" So I had to come back. You have rolls which are extremely defective. There are names which appear five times, there are names which don't appear at all, there are dead names which are still alive and there are live names which are dead. What is the percentage of defects in our rolls? This is something on which I would employ a statistician to find an answer and we have not found a true method yet of finding out how bad our rolls are. And there are places in which the entire system of election runs on rigging. All the books on election which I have and which add up to a considerable height are collectively called the Rig Veda. It has happened in a particular city where party members identify a particular multistoreyed residential building and manage to lock up the main gate on the day of the election. They create fear among the residents who want to vote for a particular party. Voters' roll, anybody?

We have impersonation which is extraordinarily widespread. Then the entire election is based upon appeals to wrong reasons. I would not expatiate on that. But appeals to wrong reasons is the basis of our elections.

I have got evidence of naked violence during the election. I have got footage after footage on violence. Somebody comes on a motorbike, and fires a country gun. Every voter runs away from the polling booth. End of the election. Capture the booth. Lack of management of law and order particularly during elections (I am not complaining against our poor brethren in uniform because they are the victims of an enormous amount of injustice), rigging, booth-capturing, violence, the absence of physical security before the election, during the election, after the election are the order of the day.

Ultimately we have a book called the *Code of Conduct*. In Britain in 1727 under Horace Walpole, they had introduced the law called the Law of Occasional Conformity. Actually though the title is misleading, everybody had to be a protestant is what the law said. We have no occasional conformity, we have no conformity to the code of conduct. If you can get away with it, that is the code of conduct. The Governor, the Minister, whoever it is, will go and open things, close things and announce all kinds of goodies, once the elections are about to start.

When I announced an election a month in advance, everybody asked me, "why are you sitting alone on this chair? You should get additional persons to work for you". I am again reverting to the title of an old English film, *Who is Afraid of Virginia Woolf?* As the poet said: "For forms of government let fools conspire, what ever is best administered is best". Ultimately we need to plug all the leaks that are prevailing in the election system. There are so many leaks and it is like a baby in acute diarrhoea bordering on dysentery. What do you give the child? According to Doordarshan, you give the child oral rehydration therapy. But by oral rehydration you cannot get rid of the disease. They said, "why does the present Election Commissioner have so many riflemen?" I'm surrounded by them because there is anger in Assam, in Bengal, in Bihar, and the respected Jyoti Basu called me 'mad dog', etc., etc. To say something about the honourable Laloo Yadav is a peril. When I asked him "please do not use government planes for election work", Yadav reportedly told *India Today*: "Does Seshan have any authority to question me?"

If you want this country to have real elections, for God's sake make the Election Commission truly autonomous. For God's sake strengthen your election machinery. Make it possible for the man to vote freely, courageously and without fear. For God's sake provide teeth for the implementation of good behaviour by political parties, whatever the country considers is good behaviour. So that is why I have said, "on the first of January 1995, nobody will go to a polling booth unless he/she has an identity card, with the photograph on it."

Make the elections free and fair. Not one, not three but 101 Election Commissioners cannot rectify the system until the people decide that you want to have a clean electoral system. When the learned Attorney-General of India argued in Parliament about me, and said the Election Commission is a subsidiary of the government, I would have liked to ask him respectfully: "Why not appoint a Director-General of Elections, who will carry out the order of the Under Secretary? The Chief Election Commissioner is equated to a Supreme Court judge. They are not prepared to accept it. But that is a different story.

You post five constables of the Central Reserve Police Force or the police in each polling station. Please multiply eight lakhs by five and tell me what number you arrive at. If you put all the policemen of India together in one basket, you do not have 40 lakh policemen. And for God's sake if you can run your election only with five of the gentlemen armed with deadly-looking weapons with their fingers on their triggers all the time, why call this a democracy? Give it some other name. As much mistakes and misdeeds are being done in elections as are possible. Shame! It is a matter of shame. You are going to run a democracy by putting five armed policemen per booth of which I have 800,000 today. And everybody says he wants elections in one day. I have no difficulty in running the election in one day. Can you give me enough protection? I'm ready to run the election in one day throughout the country, but the law and order situation of the country is such that if I do so then I will have to do what the Election Commission has been doing for the last 40 years. You look the other way when somebody says that something wrong has been done.

Everyone wants an election on a single day "because we do not want the elections at one place to influence the elections at another place". I also think in the same vein. But if you ask the Home Secretary to the Government of India, he will say, "last time I said please keep it at least four days apart, because people have to be transported from this place to that. Please keep a gap of four days between one election and the other". I told them the situation in the country is such that I would need a lot of policemen. The Government of India said I have no right to ask for policemen. That is another drama going on. It reminds me of another story. There was a beggar who came to the house, and said, "please give me alms". There was this newly married daughter-in-law standing at the door. She went to the beggar and told him in gentle tones: "Please go away, this is not a house noted for generosity." So the beggar reached the gate and the mother-in-law came to the front door and said, "who is that going away?" She said there was a beggar. "What did you tell him?" the mother-in-law thundered. "I said, they do not give alms in this house". She said to her daughter-in-law, "who are you to tell the beggar that we do not give alms. Call him back". The beggar was called back. And she said, "in this house, I have the right to say No. Not my daughter-in-law".

People asked me why I did not prevent non-serious candidates from contesting. But who is to decide whom to eliminate? I remember there was a man in Karnataka who had formed a party of which he was the leader. He was the president, he was the secretary, he was the treasurer, he was the sole member. And his party was called 'Hottepaksha'. Those of you who know a little Kannada, the word means the party of the stomach. And he stood in every election and he travelled deliberately on a donkey or a mare and said, *"Mujeh bhi vote deh do"*. He wanted to establish a record of the maximum number of defeats he has had. And today we have some gentleman like that called Kaka Joginder Singh *urf Dharti Pakad*. He sounded very good to me. But who is to decide, who is a serious candidate and who is not a serious candidate? If I can decide this, then what is the system of democracy made up of?

I do not know whether Bachi Karkaria writes nowadays. She once wrote, "Seshan is walking around railway stations cancelling trains. Just as the stationmaster shows green flags, Seshan is showing red flags all over". One paper said: "Chief Election Countermanding Commissioner".

What is the developing scenario in this country? Now what is in danger is not merely elections. What is in danger is the integrity of this country. What is at stake? I am sure our friends will say that I am a messenger of doom. I am not a messenger of doom. I am in fact an optimist. But if you do not stop this, the integrity and unity of this country will remain in danger. Instead of using non-violent peaceful means to resolve societal conflicts of money, of religion, of caste and subcaste, we are going to end up settling them by the wrong end of the knife and the wrong end of the gun. The psychological security of the future generation is at stake. What are we leaving behind for our children? I have no children, so I can speak with even greater authority. A society in which you may get 98 per cent marks, even then you will not get admission whether you are backward, you are forward, you are sideward. Or you have to bribe with seven lakhs, six lakhs, or whatever lakhs you can afford. Discontent with authority is growing to a point where even the police constable on traffic duty cannot enforce his authority. Discontent with the authority is now slowly becoming universal.

Corruption and money power are taking over everywhere. There is a developing loss of faith in the machinery for the redressal of grievance. "Something wrong has been done against me, should I go to the court? Should I go to the police station? Where do I go? Is there a guarantee that I shall get reasonable justice?" I will not answer that question. On anybody's side there is no accountability. I do not want to list all of them. What is the external manifestation of all these ills? It is societal violence. When a society cannot contain any more of its griefs and angers, it erupts in violence. I went to Kashmir in 1989 to find out what was happening. When I came back I wrote a report where I said if I were a Kashmiri I would have indulged in greater violence. I saw a room which was less than ten feet by ten feet, where ten adults including seven women were staying. The walls were made out of broken chestwood planks, which had any number of holes. The temperature in winter reached minus 15 degrees Celsius. Where would an adult girl go when nature compelled her to go? I did not have the courage to ask. If you live in a society in that kind of condition, the society is bound to break down.

"Why do we have elections?" somebody asked me. "Why do we not appoint an Idi Amin"? I do not waste time answering that question. But a true election is the only way this country can eliminate feudal vestiges, classes, castes, communities. This is the only way you can eradicate economic inequality. One of the greatest dangers in this country is the personality cult, and I should be careful before I say anything more, on fragmentation of values, division on caste, subcaste, subsubcaste and a lot more. But the fundamental roots of this loss is in moral character — the character which we inherited from Gandhiji, Sardar Patel and Nehru. No, we did not inherit it only from these people, we inherited it from Sri Rama, Sri Krishna, or we inherited it from the Parampurush in whatever religion you believe in.

There is at present an all-pervading loss of self-confidence. School students, college students come and persuade me to be their guest. "Sir, you are very good at speaking in front of the mike. Tell us what is to be done." But I have no answer to give to the poor child who says what is to be done to rectify this state of the country. It has become our national character to find fault with everybody else. Newspapers will find fault with everybody. Civil service people say the Minister is not right, and those working under him are not correct. But you point one finger at anyone, three fingers are being pointed at you.

For God's sake, let us begin by building up character. You must be thinking, "Oh, this fellow having failed in running good elections has now become a preacher. He is going to start some kind of Seshan mission." All the same, I would reiterate that unless we can improve the character of our country we would go steadily towards the path of disaster. Not the path which Gandhiji showed, which Panditji showed, which Sardar Patel showed, which several other leaders showed. As an adult society, with 5000 years of culture behind us, today we decorate ourselves with the trappings of a safari suit and forget that inside the brain, there is no ability to ask the question, what it is which ails us as a society? Until and unless we have the ability to ask this question to each and everyone of us, it matters not to me whether you vote for the hand or the lotus or two bullocks with a yoke or sickle with hammer. But where do we begin, how do we begin, who begins, what begins?

I am often accused as Seshan is so and so's man, Seshan is somebody else's man. But I am the man of 900 million people and 550 million voters. I will tell you my own story. When Mr. Chandrasekhar became the Prime Minister he first said, "you are going to be my Secretary. You are going to be Cabinet Secretary". So, for two-three days there were arguments between Chandrasekharji and Rajivji — "what shall we do with Seshan?" And somebody said, "make him Cabinet Secretary again." Somebody else said, "make him Principal Secretary to the Prime Minister". Somebody else said, "make him both." So, daily Rajiv Gandhiji early in the morning would call me and say, "Don't go back to the post of a Cabinet Secretary once again. It is not good for your self-respect. You only become the Prime Minister's Principal Secretary". He would call me in the evening and say — *"Nahin Seshan, Principal Secretary banne se faida nahin, Cabinet Secretary hi banna chahiye* So after hearing this story unnecessarily for three-four days I finally met Rajiv Gandhi and told him, "Sir, there is a fourth group. There is 'A', There is 'B'. There is 'AB.' A is Cabinet Secretary, 'B' is Principal Secretary to the Prime Minister. If you combine the two then it's 'AB'". As far as I am concerned my blood group is 'O'. So he said "Why is this topic of blood group coming in the middle of this discussion." I said 'O' is for out. But the scenario turned out to be somewhat different.

Coming back to our discussion, until the people of this country are fully awake, this country has no future. Yes, freedom and democracy will thrive on a soil of private conviction of the morally right. Last time in the Parliamentary election for 500 seats there were 9000 candidates. Average 18 plus. There is no dearth of candidates. No. Ultimately democracy will thrive in this country only on the basis of character and the voters saying enough means enough. If you do not want to have a banana republic for your next generation, then please get up and ask yourself a question: "where shall the truth come from?" I will close with a quotation from the Bible which says: "And of what shall it profit a man if he gain the whole world, but lose his soul".

2

Are We Cockroaches?

*A*re we a non-achieving society? If the answer to that question is at least partly yes, then you have to find a treatment for this, that from a non-achieving society we become an achieving society. We have been told, through generations of existence, that the most surviving animal is the ordinary household kitchen cockroach. Are we cockroaches? You can stamp on a cockroach. Five minutes later when you think it is totally dead, it suddenly turns itself upside down and runs away. I can tell you all kinds of things about the anatomy of a cockroach, I being one myself. Is survivability the fundamental of Indian existence? If I say Hindu existence, by mistake please, take my apology in advance. When I say Hindu I don't mean the people who

Speech made at the Indian Institute of Management, Ahmedabad, on 26 January 1994.

worship only Rama or Krishna or whatever else. I mean the ethos which is common to all of us. In fact, in my dictionary, *Hindutwa* means not building a temple here or destroying a mosque there. It means the ethos, the culture, the gene, the blood which runs in the veins of all of us together. And it does not matter whether you are from Punjab or from Tamil Nadu or whether you are from Kerala or from Bengal. Each of us has his own language and his own cultural hangover.

When you watch athletics, you will see that in the 1000 metres run, athletes run very well in the first 900 or 950 metres, but the last 50 metres is what the Westerner calls the "mind to kill". You may then ask, "is it desirable for somebody to have a killing trait?" If it is accepted that at least business will thrive only on the basis of a killing mentality or a killer's mentality, is it absent in us? How do we engineer it? How do they transmit it in a classroom? I asked the faculty members at the Indian Institute of Management, Ahmedabad, a question: of every hundred boys or girls who enter the institute on day one, what percentage is excellent products? The evaluation system leaves me cold. It is as good or as bad as any other evaluation system and it doesn't really produce a judgement on who is excellent. Somebody is hollow inside but is very expressive outside. Somebody has a pretty face or a good moustache and, therefore, becomes a more impressive personality. He becomes a Rambo. Now, that is not what I call excellence. In fact does this course or this institute have a niche in it to ask the question what is excellence? What constitutes excellence? For example, if I may shift to Sanskrit, *Karyakushalta* is excellence. The technical ability to do one's work better. The motto of the Indian Administrative Service is '*Yogah Karmassu Kaushalam*'. Skill in action is the ultimate in achievement. It could probably be one yardstick by which you measure excellence. Are there any other yardsticks? You may have extremely good skills but you are extremely poor in fundamental values. You have no value system at all.

Are all our ethics relative? You can certainly have relative ethics as they currently have it in the United States. They are having relative ethics on whether abortion is a good thing or a bad thing. Whether colour hatred is a good thing or a bad thing, or whether torture is a good thing or a bad thing. When this torture becomes acceptable, when this abortion becomes acceptable, when this colour conflict becomes acceptable or is it an absolute value in which you say, "come hell or high water, I am a Roman Catholic". Somebody has said that abortion is incorrect. Therefore, abortion is incorrect. A woman gets pregnant as a result of the brutal assault on her feminity. She conceives. Does she have a right to terminate the product of her humiliation or is it that it is not acceptable to have that life terminated?

Is there any inherent value? Is it right to ask the question, why are we not successful despite all that we possess? Do you think we will ever change into an achieving society? Is this achievement going to be based on amoral values or a system of values which is fundamentally amoral: it is okay to kill somebody, to get a seat it is okay to bribe somebody, to pass an exam it is okay to cheat. How much of home exercises do you cheat on, how much of plagiarism takes place from textbooks or some professor's notes which you have stacked away. I see an enveloping gloom all over the place.

Every single major or minor admission in India is based on corruption. That is the condition of your education. That is the condition of your health. There are States in which copying is being actively encouraged. Now how much would you like to go and let a doctor inject you, leave alone cut you open, on the basis of a degree obtained by copying. Engineers build bridges and buildings which keep crashing repeatedly. The same can be said of lawyers, judges, IAS officers, politicians, teachers, students. I have been, since the last four years, searching for one square foot of this country which is made up of dry sand. I am not talking of the

Rajasthan desert. I am looking for dryness which is not impregnated with corruption. Why are question papers leaked? Why do only children who take tuition from the class teacher pass? Why is valuation bogus? A child comes and weeps deplorably to the mother or the father saying, "these are not my marks. It cannot be". And to get your answer paper revalued, it needs *sifhaarish*. What price this education? Admission? Examination? What happens in the civil services? Can you get anything done without 'speed money'? Can you get anything done in the processes of law without 'speed money'? Two lawyers will agree on both sides and they will apply for adjournment. One would say, "Your Lordship, I am having a stomach ache, let's have this next week, or a week after" and he is going to tell his client, "*Main itna lara, aap key liye itna lara*. Please produce Rs. 10,000 which is my fees."

Justice in this country has comprehensively collapsed. Be it at the hands of police or at the hands of lawyers. In any case whether it is a small case, medium case, large case, it wouldn't be heard for years. By then you have died, your son has died, your grandson alone is available. Justice anybody? Law anybody? Electricity anybody? Telephone anybody? If you dial a number there is a cross-connection. You can hear abuses and romantic talks on the cross-connection — you can hear all kinds of things. But you can't get Ahmedabad or any other place. We have 'satellite telephone lines' but can't get one suburb of Ahmedabad from another. If you ask the Telephone Department, "what is the percentage of successful telephone call?" they will say 99.999. That is the percentage of calls satisfactorily completed as if you and I do not know the reality of the situation.

There is not much to talk about bus transport, rail transport and the airlines which publishes a time-table for the sole purpose of enabling you to determine how many hours late you are. Talking of railways, there used to be a time when we had a Minister called Lal Bahadur Shastri who resigned because one train jumped off the track. Today a train jumping off the track is a daily occurrence. But somebody else will say, "but the PM did not ask me to resign. That is why I am not resigning." What price morality in this country? What price responsibility in this country? What passes for democracy? Is it based upon the quicksands of non-moral irresponsibility? You can find an excuse for anything which has happened in this place and declare, "this is not my responsibility. I have not been directly accused". Then what kind of democracy are you talking about? What kind of country are you talking about? *Sare jehan se achha Hindustan hamara*!

You may accuse me of causing despair. But look at the corruption in science and technology. Across the length and breadth of the country people who pass for managers are not managers, people who pass for scientists are not scientists, people who pass for lawyers are not lawyers, people who pass for administrators are not administrators. There is no point in hiding the injury inside the body from the doctor. Doctors can't treat you if you don't expose the wound or expose the itch or the infection. So I am exposing the infection at the moment all over the country. I want you to ask the question: "Do we need to clean up this country?" Now, where do we start cleaning this up? You are willingly being exposed to activities which you don't know how to deal with. You deal with the private sector where industry was completely protected. Even *Falana* soap was protected (I have nothing against *Falana* soap, I used to use it as a youngster). But today a foreign soap may arrive. What will you do? How are you going to be exposed to international competition? You can't even make a lousy TV set. You go and give phoney acronym to products. You say "this is the only refrigerator with ABC".

Their lordships said from the supremacy of a High Court bench or a Supreme Court bench that the only thing that doesn't make noise in an Indian car is the horn. It was said years ago about the Hindustan car. When you talk of excellence, what price quality? What price quality under internationally cut-throat competitive circumstances? Will you still sell soaps in a protected market? The best organisational behaviour you could have taught any group of management students 10 years ago was to distinguish between the preferences of senior civil servants, between black label and blue label. I am talking the harsh truth? But I am trained to speak the harsh truth.

It's so agonising. You are so near, yet you are so far. For years together you had third-rate people, fourth-rate people as Chief Ministers, Prime Ministers. Along came somebody called Rajiv Gandhi. Everybody fell for his face until he got sucked into the system from which he never came out. In December 1986, he made a speech in Bombay at the AICC session on power-brokers. Four months later the power-brokers had sucked him in. All the charisma was destructed in Sriperambudur in the fleeting might of an explosive. Where and how do we create heroes? How does the system throw up heroes? Heroes in management, heroes in sports, heroes in business, heroes in administration, heroes in politics? Would somebody in the Institute of Management, Ahmedabad, please set time and effort apart to tell me how to create excellence. In particular, how to create excellence in managers. We produce managers who are by and large excellent. How does it matter? They are just like Alice in Wonderland; they change the rules to suit the managers. Are you producing managers who are of world class excellence? Are you producing managers for a changing ambience, for a changing atmosphere, a changing *mahaul*, in which all the old rules, in terms of management have to be rewritten?

Why is it that India cannot produce a single world class Olympic gold medallist in any branch of athletics? Why can't it produce a Nobel Prize winner of the level of Hargovind Khurana, who was awarded not because he was an Indian but because he was in the States. Rabindranath Tagore had certainly nothing to do with our education system or Institute of Management whether at Ahmedabad, or Calcutta or anywhere else. He produced poetry despite all other things.

What is it that will produce excellence in this country? What is it that we should do to clean up this mess?

Everybody agrees that one's life is in a mess. Gas is a mess, bus is a mess, car is a mess, phone is a mess, admission is a mess, even copying is a mess. Copying is a mess because if the teacher finds out you have copied, the director will give him a chit saying "you ought to have been more tactful". Isn't that true? If IIM Ahmedabad is excellent, what are you doing to preserve this island of excellence? If it is true that you are excellent, what medicine are you applying, are you applying radiation therapy or are you applying something else by which once people enter this area they all turn into *Shud Vanaspati*. The moment they go out they turn into *milavat hi milavat*. These are the questions which bother us.

Every member of Parliament or an Assembly without exception utters a lie before he takes the oath by saying, "I have kept my election expenses within the law". What does the law say? The law says 'ordinarily resident'. So shall I apply relative values to say that India should not lose an outstanding Finance Minister or shall I apply fundamental values that anybody who breaks the law is the breaker of the law be he ever so great. Where will you deal with this kind of mental agony? In everyone of us, in every part of life, there will be certain fundamental values which you 'rub' but if it shows up less than 24 carats, then what do you do?

The foundation of our nation is broken. A society or community based on as much injustice as we are in is unlikely to succeed. Injustice not in the court of law. Injustice in the sense that there is no court to which you can convey a sense of grief. You will be going around, head lowered, shoulders stooped speaking out the dictum, *"Karega kya."* You can't get a gas cylinder until your wife threatens to throw the *chapati* pan at your face. Then you go and pay somebody Rs. 85 plus Rs. 25 for early delivery. And he will give you 10 kilos instead of the 14 kilos and you can't ask questions. Corruption has become so widespread in this country that I challenge anyone of you to say this area is clean. This square foot of land is available from which we can expand the dry area. We can start expanding the dry area in the rest of the country from Kashmir to Kanyakumari, from Kathiavad to Kamrup.

I was reading a poster today. It said, *Hindi main kaam karna aasan hai. Shuru to kijiye.* Why put it on my car number plate? When I am hit by a car I would not be able to read the car number. Everybody in this country except a small number of Hindi pundits has been rendered illiterate because we can't read the number on the car number plates. What does your law say about the use of Hindi as official language? It says when Hindi is used as the official language, the numerals used should be of the international form of the Indian numerals. And when I get the pin code of your Director's letter, that is in Devnagari numerals. I have no problem. You have all kinds of mass communication institutes talking of subliminal transfer of information. How will you do your transfer of information? Is it by MTV, is it by Zee TV or will you do it with the ATN? But ultimately, language is the means of correspondence of communication, thoughts and ideas. We have a gentleman mentioned in a South Indian story who sat on a branch of a tree and was cutting the bottom of the branch. Why are you doing the same thing to my language? How does it matter if one communicates in Hindi or English or Gujarati or in any other language? Ultimately, we must learn to talk to each other. Today, we are cutting the branches of our trees while sitting on the same branches. The branches, along with all of us, will one day fall down.

Today in all the educational institutions there is a students' union owing affinity to this or that party. Elections in universities are fought on the basis of parties spending Rs. 20 lakhs, Rs. 50 lakhs, Rs. 60 lakhs. So, somebody accused me of having made the mistake of giving the children of today the right to vote at the age of 18 when they are not mature enough. The children on the contrary are asking me, "if we are mature enough to vote at 18, why can't be we members of Parliament at 18?" I want to come back to the basic point and, that is, one is always in a state of agony because your elected representatives represent nothing. What do they represent, whom do they represent other than themselves? Shall I give you the 360 degrees of my agony? The roads are bad, the polling stations are bad. The political parties are playing hockey on the cricket field. The civil servant has a broken backbone. Today each Indian civil servant, from the Chief Secretary down to the *thanedar*, if he wants to be honest, his back is broken repeatedly. "Under such circumstances, how will you improve the civil service of India?" Please go and get the best orthopaedic surgeon and ask him to set right his broken backbone.

"Who broke them?" I want to point an accusing finger at you and say, "you broke them". "Why, how did we break them? It is the Minister who broke them." No. When the Minister was breaking the back of an honest civil servant, you were sitting by and watching idly. A civil servant learnt from a person who sat up, or stood up for the truth to be first a collaborative, then to a collusive, committed and then finally to being an accomplice kind of a civil servant. Who will answer for this? You will now ask me, "Sir, will you honestly tell me that when you were in the civil service for 36 years, were you also not a polished call girl?" Yes, I was, but I was mostly unpolished. I used to be crude. Who broke the system? Why did the masses of India not stand up and say if somebody is trying to fight for the enforcement of the ordinary rights of an ordinary individual, he needs to be protected. How many people will stand up to protect a civil servant doing an honest job today? In which part of India? So do I hold too many accusing fingers? Does it hurt? Does it make you angry?

The cleaning up process must start from *Panchayati Raj* which we had 3000 years ago. Panditji started a *Panchayati Raj* Movement in the late fifties. Within less than 10 years, it had been comprehensively snuffed out by a corrupt political set-up aided and abetted by the civil service who saw their rights of control going away. Another *Panchayati Raj* is beginning today. The result is obvious. What will it end up in? It will end up in small VIP suitcases. It will end up in vomitting liquor on the floor of Parliament. It will end up by people being purchased. "So why don't you give us a law by which people who cross floors can be declared no longer MPs?" Don't ask me, I am an umpire. Give me a new offside rule and I will blow the whistle for you. But don't ask me why there is no law. You get the law passed. You ask for it. You insist on it. Because no amount of pontification by me will produce one iota of result unless you rise up. But don't rise up and burn buses and smash glasses. Rise up and tell the people who matter, "this we won't agree with."

Protecting democracy! Who will protect it? The Chief Election Commissioner? The Election Commission of India with or without two extra Commissioners? Or maybe with another hundred extra Commissioners? A hundred Election Commissioners would not give this to you. I am not saying this because I am the 101st. There can be a hundred more laws. Somebody will get up and say, "Sir, why can't we have proportional representation by the single transferable vote" or "why can't we have a list system? Germany has a list system". I'll repeat what I say everywhere. Models look good. But only on the catwalk.

In the whole of human history there has been no greater joke than the Indian election account expenses limit. Extra expenses incurred by others on my behalf should not be questioned. Everybody else, my brother is spending, my sister is spending, my father is spending, my enemy is spending, I spent only Rs. 2522. Every single member of Parliament is allowed to enter its portals after uttering a technological inexactitude (as Churchill would have said, on the floor of Parliament, in order that somebody would not say he used the word 'lies' which is unparliamentary). But Churchill told Parliament that right honourable members' opinion is a technological inexactitude. Every single member of Parliament walks in with reverence. Some put their hands on the steps and put them on their heads. But inside they give me an accounts statement which is the world's greatest joke.

What is the fundamental source of corruption in India? Human greed, certainly. But much more than human greed, the thing which has institutionalised corruption in India, like nothing else has, is money power which goes to the elections of this country, which then takes you to the seat of power and authority where you can dispense life and death to hundreds and thousands and millions of people. "So what are you doing about it?" Don't ask me. Either you give me the whistle or you find somebody else to do it for you. You have not given me the whistle. Today there is a section in the law which says that money spent by others need not be taken into account while submitting bills, or statement of account. Can you ban company donations to parties? Have you thought of a greater joke than this?

You will now realise that what passes for democracy is not democracy. It does not have any of the elements of democracy. There is no will of the people. There is no rule by the will of the people. There is no rule by consent. There is no administration of justice, much less is there any equality in the eyes of the law as far as all people are concerned. For the ordinary man whether you call him 'dalam', PWG or Naxalite or something else, in different parts of the country, the country is seeing a loss of faith in that which passes for democracy. We don't know what we fought for.

But we are not getting what we fought for. I accuse you of having engineered the kind of democracy which is a sham, which is rubbish, which is useless, and which no longer gives any kind of satisfaction to anybody.

The only protection for democracy in this country is not a much better Chief Election Commissioner, it doesn't need several more of them. The country can afford to have a *panchayat* of Election Commissioners. It doesn't need more laws, because a new law will never be implemented and by chance if it becomes effective it will be altered overnight. Why don't you abolish Articles 324 to 329 of the Constitution and appoint a Director-General of Elections who will report to the Under Secretary, Election Department? People in this country must understand that those in power never leave power whether they are here by election or by appointment. Have you ever heard of anybody relinquishing power after Shri Rama? Shri Rama is the only last known instance of somebody relinquishing power voluntarily. Because his father gave a boon to his mother, or his father's second wife because she put her finger into the axle of his chariot when he was about to lose the battle. That is why in Valmiki's Ramayana when Rama goes to take leave of his mother, she says:

Yat palayasi dharmam tvam
Daityena niyamēna cha
Sa vai Raghava sārdoola
Dharman Twaam abhirakshatu

I want to mention this to you with pain, with grief, that the average man and woman of our country has failed India completely.

Three hundred years ago we were a great country. Hopefully 20 years from now we will again be a great country. It is not going to become great by sitting and saying Rama did this, Krishna did this or Chola did that. Give yourself a pat on your back saying my great grandfather said this was the country where milk and honey were flowing. But it won't come back. Yet I would come back to the rhetoric *sare jehan se achha Hindustan hamara*. India has this possibility of greatness. India has extraordinary facilities. It has got places with 500 inches of rain. It has got deserts. It has got snow. It has got Narmada river whether you dam it or you don't dam it. You have got power by the millions of kilowatts. You have culture, you have art, and you have brain, and you have everything. But wisdom to run this by yourself is missing. And if I say this sitting where I do, I don't say you alone are responsible because when I point one finger at you, three fingers are pointing at me. All of us are collectively responsible for the tragic pass to which we have brought this country. I want to apologise if I have conveyed to you a mood of desperation. I have a mood of agony, not of desperation. I have a mood of solemnity not of anguish. I have a mood of helplessness, not frustration.

3

A Conspiracy of Silence

I am deeply grateful to you for giving me this opportunity of talking to a group of people who are essentially closest to God. I say this, because if there is one vision in which the human being can see closest to God, it is justice and the rule of law. Of all the attributes which you attribute to the God of your choice, you attribute him with affection, with various other qualities, but I think ultimately in the heart of every devoted person the concept is that whatever else God may or may not give him, that God will certainly render him justice. That is the basis on which almost all of us have been nurtured in the belief of a God who is benign, who is friendly, who may be harsh in the short run but in the medium to long run is absolutely neutral and full of justice, tempered with compassion.

Address at Lucknow Lawyers' Forum on 9 May 1994.

Therefore, I consider the opportunity of talking to this Lawyers' Forum a very great advantage. The advantage has been both multiplied and made frightening by the presence of distinguished members of high judiciary in the audience. For 36 years I was a civil servant and all that I learnt was that one respected the judiciary totally, unquestioningly, completely, always ever. And it need not have to be the Supreme Court, it need not have to be a High Court, it could even be a district court or a subordinate court in the district, but the law was the law and, therefore, there is no question of not respecting it.

I don't know where to begin. The organisers of the meeting have suggested to me to speak on the Model Code and Its Implementation. But I have to request you to bear with me when I say, please allow me to extend this not only to the Model Code but to all that goes into the manner of running elections in India. Model Code is only one small part of it. There are other parts of it which need to be dilated upon, dealt with, albeit fleetingly, in order to give us the full taste and texture of that which now seems to be as if it is a brand new item. Almost as if a multimember Election Commission is a brand new item. People in this country forget that the possibility of a multimember Commission was envisaged not in 1989 by Mr. Rajiv Gandhi nor in 1993 by the present Government. It was envisaged when the original Constitution was written, when it said that the Election Commission of India shall consist of the Chief Election Commissioner and such other Commissioners or Regional Commissioners (I am putting it in common language not in the exact verbatim reproduction of the Article of the Constitution) as the President may from time to time appoint. When I say additional Election Commissioners or extra Election Commissioners (any one of the appellations would be objected to by my distinguished colleagues in the Commission) I say it in a small 'a' or a small 'e' sense. Not that they are Additional Commissioners, they are as much

Commissioners as I am. If the newspapers have to be believed, they are going to be equated in every way with the Chief Election Commissioner. Be that as it may.

I have had the good fortune of reading through extensively the debates in the Constituent Assembly while introducing the portions constituting the Election Commission by incorporating Articles 324 to 329 into the Constitution. I won't expatiate upon it except to say that what the founding fathers had in mind was an Election Commission which was independent of the entire executive, but certainly not independent of the benign protective control, protective not only of itself but the rights of everybody else against an abuse of such extraordinary powers as are vested in the Commission. Then it said that the Election Commission shall be responsible for the superintendence, direction and control of the elections in India — elections to the State legislatures, elections to the two Houses of Parliament, elections to the office of the Vice-President of India, election to the office of the President of India.

Before I go into the comparatively limited question of the Model Code of Conduct and some of the other things which have brought an arrow to my chest, I want to tell you about what has happened to Indian elections in a manner in which they look, from Nirvachan Sadan. If you are sitting on a High Court bench or looking at it with the robes of a lawyer, I am sure it will look different. If you are looking at it from the pen of a pressman, it, I am sure, will look different. From the point of view of an ordinary person, it will give yet another kind of angle or view. But looking at it from the Election Commission's point of view, no, I can't say Election Commission's point of view, but *my* point of view in the Election Commission, I want to mention to you that the elections in Indian today are a comprehensive joke.

Sitting in this chair of responsibility, how can I say this? How can I not say this? Isn't it appalling that the Chief Election Commissioner of India should take the courage to say this? If I did not say this I would not have been worthy of any trust. Today, I have 550 million voters in the voters' list — 55 crores of them, with a total population of approximately 90 crores. A population, which in A.D. 2001, the demographers have told us without doubt, will cross a billion people. And there will be a voters' list of approximately 60 per cent, which is always a reasonable number. Our population is growing at the rate of two-and-a-half per cent per year and if you erect a demographic pyramid you will notice that the number of children below the age of 18 is growing further and further, larger and larger. Voters' lists are full of holes. There are dead people still on the rolls. There are live people not on the rolls. There are people who are on the rolls in many places by accident, by mistake. There are people who are on rolls in many places by deliberate design and effort. There are parts of India in which people are deliberately omitted from the rolls. There is one part of India where they say anybody who lives in a multistoreyed building is *ipso facto* not our friend and, therefore, his name ought not to be on the rolls. You don't need too much time to guess in which part of the country this is done. But I shall *not* name that State. Today after a revision conducted in 1993, what we call an intensive revision of house-to-house enumeration, we are close to touching upon 800,000 — eight lakh polling booths throughout the country. In many cases these are located with a deliberate view to prevent those who are socially and economically weak from coming to vote. The polling booths are located by a deliberate collusion between the political executive and the civil service executive at locations which render it not only difficult but impossible for the weak and the poor to get into the polling booth.

Is impersonation reasonable? No, it is not reasonable. The other day I was in a constituency in Maharashtra, a constituency with a million voters of which a total voter turn-out was 68 per cent, and the total number of impersonators captured by the police was exactly two. Without meaning to cast aspersions on anybody, those two impersonation cases of 1989 are still under processing.

While the elections are going on, all kinds of evil methodologies are resorted to. Not yesterday or day before yesterday, the delimitation of constituencies was a matter of bargain in order to make sure that this community or that community, this caste or that caste has a decisive majority in the number of voters in that constituency. I shall not go back into the working of the Delimitation Commission which has not sat since the last 20 years; Parliament by law has laid down that until the population figures of A.D. 2001 were available there will be no further delimitation. This is said to be in support of the family welfare or family planning programme, that no delimitation would be done again till A.D. 2000. That is the rule or law in the Statute Book at the moment. I have read it along with some of you in the newspapers that Parliament is in the process of altering it to the 1991 census. It also says Parliament is in the process of amending the law to make sure that there is a rotation of seats reserved for scheduled castes and tribes so that the same constituency does not continue as a reserved seat for the next 20 years, 30 years or 40 years.

If you look at the newspapers, while an election is on, you will see a strange spectacle of somebody saying seat number 'A' is decisively of so and so caste majority constituency. Seat number 'B' is decisively so and so caste majority constituency. Seat number 'C' is of so and so majority. Then the parties set up candidates in order to make sure that maximum allowance, maximum gain can be made of the fact that the given constituency has a majority of voters from a given caste or community, or religion whatever you call it. Casteless, classless, secular state anybody? So that is the delimitation, that is the constituency. Speeches are made as if some of the laws in the Statute Book of India did not exist at all. Somebody stands up in the capital of India and says people of the following persuasion will be stabbed and thrown into the Yamuna. We have an audio, video recording of the incident. But the government will not take any action. Secular society anybody?

It is not for the Election Commission to take action on this. It is not something which happens only at election time. It is happening round the year, whether it is a five-year cycle, four-year cycle or three-year cycle or whatever is your cycle now. It is happening round the year and there is a tremendous conspiracy of silence. Just as a cat which closes its eye and believes nobody is watching would drink the milk by stealth, nobody is watchful while speeches are made by all kinds of people which are so inflammatory in content. I am not talking of people of kind 'A' or kind 'B' or kind 'C', they are all of the same kind as far as I am concerned.

What else is wrong with the elections? If I have said that the political parties of India play elections on the basis of playing hockey on the cricket field, would you consider me guilty of exaggeration? What kinds of methods are not adopted? To prevent the honest voters from coming in, bombs, country-made guns, *khathas* are frequently used. There are large parts in this country where eligible women voters have never reached the polling booths in the last 40 years even once. When a certain Chief Minister said that in the 1993 November elections, many women of that community did manage to reach the polling booths, I immediately suffered from a dislocated shoulder joint by patting myself on the back. We call this a democracy? People are intimidated, bombs are used, threats are held out and the counting would be done in such a way that every booth could be identified as to which political party it voted for and after the election each of these booths or the villages is attacked, the slums burnt down, people picked up under all kinds of oppressive laws relating to the freedom of the rights of the individual. All this was done because the only crime was that the ladies and gentlemen of that village voted in a particular way.

What kind of abuse is not used during an election? Somebody referred to the question of financial limits of expenditure, I did not play them down. The rule relating to the limit of expenditure being Rs. 50,000 approximately for an Assembly seat and somewhere between 1.5 and 2 lakhs for a Parliament seat is made by Government and it was fixed when petrol was selling at Rs. 6 or 7 to a litre compared to Rs. 18 per litre last year and Rs. 20 a litre today. It was laid down when everything cost one-third of what it is today. Plenty of applications from every single distinguished predecessor of mine, Peri Shastri, Trivedi, Shakhder have been filed to say "please change this rule". But it has fallen on deaf ears. In the meantime, Parliament so very kindly amended Section 77 of the Representation of the People Act and said, "expenditures incurred by friends and parties need not be taken into account".

What can the Election Commission do about it? It makes sure that election account expense statement submitted is in the form prescribed. What is written inside does not concern him (CEC). If he knows that today there is a sitting member of Parliament who has spent eight crores compared to the two lakhs prescribed as the ceiling, the Chief Election Commissioner can proceed to learn to blow the *shehnai*. He can do nothing else. I am willing to stick my neck out and say that *every single member or every single legislature* in India walks into the august building after telling a lie that I spent Rs. 250 on my nomination and Rs. 213 on all the other things put together. But you conducted at least a hundred public meetings? How did you put up the dais and how did you put up the mike and in some cases how did you bring the audience? The audience is also slightly expensive. When inflation was single digit, it used to be Rs. 5 per head, now that rate has become Rs. 50. I know in Delhi the compulsory audience which is obtained costs Rs. 50 per head. Also there is the compulsory non-paying use of the buses of the State transport.

How many posters did you print? The other day, I wanted to print posters for an entertainment show for my *sabha* or association, and I was told that each two-colour poster will cost Rs. 20. True, if you have to print them in thousands and thousands, you would probably get a concession. Even then paper is paper, print is print. You can't get two-colour posters for less then Rs. 10 per poster. In a constituency I saw at least 50,000 posters. If each costs Rs. 10 and then include the cost of sending it to the villages and have somebody put gum on the rear side and paste it on some unsuspecting individual's wall or the PWD engineers' office's name plate or wherever you put it, how much does the total expenditure come to? Everybody in the country knows that on an election day every single adult in that area is given either a bottle or, now, in modern technology, a polythene bag of liquor. In every constituency women are treated to a piece of textile. In many constituencies the younger people who don't have votes are fed good wholesome food.

The other day, there was a by-election in which *every* single woman voter, half a million of them, for a Parliament seat was given a *nath,* i.e., a nose ring. Shall we say for the sake of argument that it was made of 200 mg, not even 1 gram. It was not 22-carat gold, it was not 20-carat gold, maybe it was 14-carat, because as a student of physics I know that if you make it 12-carat the gold will break. So it cannot be below 14-carat. So will you please calculate the cost of half a million *naths* of 200 mg each of 14-carat gold? What price is truth in this country? You amend the law to say that the Election Commission shall only go into making sure that the form is all right. It is the written law of the country today. I am not pulling something out of my head and presenting it to you. It's all written in the Representation of the People Act.

Today, elections in India — and I have said this through the length and breadth of the country — are based on cash, criminality and corruption. Nothing else.

What did the previous Chief Election Commissioners do? They were gentlemen.

"What are you?" You decide for yourself whether I am a '*Khalnayak*'? Whether I am an 'Alseshan' (Alsatian)? whether I am a 'mad dog'? These are names given to me by hon'ble Chief Ministers running across the length and breadth of this country. One Chief Minister called me 'insane lunatic'. I went to him and said, "Sir, is this really true? Are there sane lunatics and insane non-lunatics?" *Aap jis nam se pukarna chahate ho pukaro, hamein koi itraj nahin hai.* There is nothing more comprehensively dishonest an exercise in this country than the basis on which we elect.

Why are elections so expensive? Everybody will say "because the poorest people must be able to come and represent the people in Parliament and the Assemblies." Which poor person, which honest person, which person known for integrity in the community, of character, of honesty, of compassion, how many of them have reached the Houses of law-making in the last 20 years? If my answer is the same as yours and your answer is the same as mine, why is this so? There was a time when you needed cash, before you needed corruption. Sometimes we needed the assistance of criminals for doing these works of collecting. After some time the criminals said, "why do I assist you, I can go and sit myself." So they have. I didn't say this, the national newspapers of India said that out of 425 members in the Uttar Pradesh Assembly 180 were history-sheeters. I did a little survey on that. I think the record-holder is one MLA in Uttar Pradesh with 21 FIRs under Section 302. Who am I to tell how Assemblies should be run, how Parliament should be run? They will get angry with me, they will summon me for contempt of privilege or whatever else, but is it permissible for an ordinary voter or tax-payer to ask whether the microphones in the UP Assembly building were not intended to be thrown at each other. In December 1993 when the Assembly met for the first time, 75 out of 80 mikes were pulled out of their stands and thrown at each other. Several members came out, not like a Bombay film shooting where tomato juice does the business for blood, but with real blood streaming down their faces. They were bleeding for the country! What kind of democracy are you talking about?

They say "Seshan is a nigger in the woodpile who has arrived and is asking inconvenient questions." I pleaded with you, don't put me in this chair, I will be an inconvenient liability. You did not agree. Now they say you have removed 7.5 lakh Bangladeshis from the roads in Assam. Therefore, they are angry. When the Chief Minister of a State was using the official helicopter for electioneering work, I asked him, "is this fair?" At which he asked me "*kis haisieth se*"?

The Chief Minister of Andhra said the election was not "between me and Renuka Chowdhry, it was between me and Seshan. Mr. Seshan referred every petition from every Tom, Dick and Harry for answer." A gentlemen by the name of N.T. Rama Rao is the President of the Telugu Desam, National President of the National Front. Would you prefer to call him Tom, Dick or Harry?

My tale of happiness is inexhaustible. But I want to mention something. I have sat in counting halls where committed civil servants have counted votes saying '67, 68, 69, 40'. I have seen it and heard it with my own eyes and ears '37, 38, 39, 60'. In Bihar, the other day we found a ballot box with 700 votes tied with a rubber band. How did it go in? Must be by some kind of *jadu*. In one constituency in Bihar 100 per cent of polling was completed at 7.15 a.m. As many as 800 votes had been polled between 7 a.m. and 7.10 a.m. In yet another constituency in Bihar, in a strong room where the boxes were kept pending for counting, the collector-cum-returning officer opened the room without telling anybody, either me or the Election Commission or the local political parties. What did he do inside? I wouldn't know. When I asked him, "*Bhai kya ho raha hai?*" He said there was a deaf and dumb man who was also locked up inside along with the boxes and he was scratching the door to be let out. I am not giving you apocryphal stories. These are all written down. I have got documentation. Is there one single way in which we don't damage our elections? "So T.N. Seshan introduced the Model Code"? It is a widely held view. I greatly regret to say it is not true. They put out a new edition in 1991. I was an innocent fellow in the office for ten days. They said, "please sign it, the new issue is being issued". So I put my signature to it. That is my total contribution to the Model Code. Please remember, the Model Code was not done by me. It was not done by Peri Shastri, it was not done by Trivedi. I think Shakhdar's stand is that it was issued after elaborate meetings with all the parties. The Model Code *is* the Model Code. It doesn't have a statutory backing, but that is obvious, isn't it? If it had statutory backing rules, we won't call it a Model Code, we would have said, section so-and-so of the RP Act or it is in so-and-so of the Article of the Constitution or whatever else is appropriate to quote.

The Model Code has six or seven parts. I will tell you the headings of the parts, not the whole of the order. General conduct. Don't go and abuse somebody's grandfather and his heritage. Don't use corrupt practices. Don't use somebody else's land or building or wall without his permission. Don't create obstructions to other people's meetings. Do unto other people's meetings as you would have them do unto you. Hold meetings in the following ways. Hold processions in the following ways. In the polling booth, please don't enter without a valid pass. If you were to send observers, please assist them. Please don't take away all the rooms in the dak-bungalow. Please don't announce all loan write-offs after election is announced. Don't misuse government aircraft. Don't combine election work with official work. Don't issue advertisements at the cost of the public exchequer to say what your party in power has done. Don't sanction grants and what not unless it is on humanitarian ground. Ministers and others shall not announce financial grants, shall not lay foundation stones, shall not make any promise of construction of new facilities, shall not make *ad hoc* appointments. Ministers shall not enter a polling station or a place of counting except in their capacity as a candidate or an authorised agent.

This is the Model Code of Conduct. There is no more to it, no less to it. I still don't know why everybody is saying that Seshan has newly founded the Model Code. It is like the newspapers, writing "government has found a new method of multimember commission". It is in the original Constitution of India. Till 1989 nobody found it necessary to use this. In 1989, the then Prime Minister decided that the Election Commission was so heavily overworked that he needed to send two persons to assist Peri Shastry in the form of S.S. Dhanoa and Seigel.

"Where were you?"

I was Cabinet Secretary.

"What did you do?" I did nothing; I knew nothing till I saw it in the newspapers with you.

The less said about it the better. They were appointed after Parliament had thrown out the Panchayati Raj Constitution Amendment Bill, for which purpose the additional members were being sent to the Election Commission. So the next Government came on the 2nd of December, 1989. By February-March they told these gentlemen, "please go home and live happily ever after". One of them took it to the Supreme Court. But the Supreme Court passed the judgement, which I should not quote because it will be too long. But it only said the Chief Election Commissioner is not *primus inter pares*.

The new Government passed the Panchayati Raj Constitution Amendment Bill 73 or 74 and they appointed State Election Commissions. India is now going to have 26 Election Commissions. One plus 25. Each State is going to have its own Election Commission. I shall not comment on them because it is outside my turf. I have gone on record during the last two or three years that on an average I don't have more than 10 minutes' work a day. If you can find somebody in some place who will tell me that the Election Commission is not sending a reply, the Election Commission is not responding to the State Government's request for this or that to be approved, the Election Commission is not pursuing its cases vigorously enough in the court, if you find fault with me for anything at all, I shall accept it. Nobody has been able to find that and yet, they found it necessary to strengthen the Election Commission by sending two additional members, two extra members, not that they are extra commissioners. But they are Commissioners. And they are extra to the Chief Election Commissioner.

And what did they do on 1st October? The matter is *sub-judice*, and so I will be careful in what I say. An ordinance is passed to amend, do you know which section? The Constitution says, if you read Articles 324 to 329, "Parliament may by law lay down the procedure to conduct election". Parliament may by law lay down the terms and conditions of service of the Chief Election Commissioner and other Election Commissioners. There is nothing else in the Constitution which says Parliament may by law lay down how the Commission runs itself. So in the Act relating to the terms and conditions of service of the Chief Election Commissioner and the other Election Commissioners, an ordinance is passed, of which Sections 1 to 8 say these gentlemen will also draw Rs. 9000, these gentlemen will also live for six years, these gentlemen will also have the status of a Supreme Court judge, etc. Section 9, again in common garden language, states that functioning of the Commission shall be governed according to the next section. The next section says, the work of the Commission shall be divided and the procedure shall be adopted by a unanimous decision of the Commission. All decisions shall be taken by consensus and if there is no consensus, it shall be done by majority. Do you know where this appears? It appears in the law relating to the terms and conditions of service of the Chief Election

Commissioner and the other Election Commissioners. If I have gone to the Supreme Court to question the vires of this law I hope there will be somebody who says that I am not entirely bereft of either wisdom or legal advice. The matter is before their lordships, their lordships have referred this to the Constitution Bench, and saying anything more at the moment would be utterly impertinent and I shall be guilty of the most abonimable offence. I shall speak no more.

"Why have you treated these two Commissioners shabbily?"

It is public knowledge, I had filed a writ. They were appointed on 1st of October. They landed in office the day I was in Pune on a private visit. The rest of the staff were holding a meeting to condole the deaths in the Lattur earthquake. That very day these two gentlemen arrived very symbolically, very appropriately. Then, I was told, "please cut your leave short and come back". But I said, "the Constitution provides for extra Commissioners, how does it matter, why should I come back?" I also said, "give them all the respect and courtesy that is their due". To make a long story short we have spent only Rs. 8.5 lakhs in furnishing the rooms of those two people. I have no business to grudge it. They have also spent another Rs. 3.5 lakhs on buying two staff cars for them. Of course, they should. On the 11th, I called for a first informal/formal meeting. It was not informal in the sense that it was done on a telephone. It was not formal in the sense that there was an agenda. There is a one-line letter from me saying "may we meet on Monday, the 11th of October at 11 a.m.?"

One of my distinguished colleagues walked into the room and for the next 45 minutes, he abused me in the choicest words which dictionaries cannot find. Mr. Ghali Venkatagopala Krishnamurthy abused me for 45 minutes. My total contribution at the end of the 45 minutes was, when he said, "what happens now?" To that I said, "the meeting is over". Did I tape it? No, it is contrary to my ethics to call a colleague to my room and tape him without his knowledge.

Newspaper after newspaper remarked, "Seshan refuses to allot work to other Commissioners". You passed a law which says the allocation of work and the procedures should be determined unanimously by the Commission. So I wrote to them. The only reply I got was, "let us meet every morning at 11 o'clock". I can present it before any court of competent jurisdiction. Is that allocation of work or a procedure? I would like somebody to tell me.

Somebody told me, "you are working against national integrity". What he meant was integration. But it is a different matter that his English let him down. I don't know what the founding fathers of the Constitution decided. Was this role to be played by the Rajya Sabha with regard to the running of the country? I have read the Constitution and the Representation of the People Act very carefully. It says, no one may represent a State in the Rajya Sabha unless he is an elector in that State. Why is this important that he represent the State? I found at least one Article which is fundamental to the genesis of the whole picture where Article 1 of the Constitution states that India shall be a Union of States. India that is Bharat shall not be divided into States. Article 249 gives authority to take away the functions of the State under the Sixth Schedule into the hands of the Central Government and Parliament for one year at a time, not with Lok Sabha votes, but the Rajya Sabha votes. Would it be correct for me to point out to you that under the Constitution, any function of the State Government may be taken over by the Central Government if a resolution is passed in the Rajya Sabha. If you pass that resolution in the Lok Sabha which is the house of the people, it doesn't help. It must be passed in the Rajya Sabha.

I am an extinguished bureaucrat. I know no law. "Why do you want to chase this up?" Because I am paid to chase this up. I have found a 150 things wrong with the Indian elections. From voters' rolls down to accounts, etc. Two and a half years ago, I had the good fortune of meeting the Prime Minister on an occasion. I said, "I suffer acutely for want of work, is there something which you would suggest that I do? So my successor doesn't come and say this fool went on saying he doesn't have enough work, why could he not have done this?" The Prime Minister was good enough to suggest "send your comprehensive electoral reforms proposals". So I sent them on 10 February 1992. As of May 1994, I don't have an acknowledgement. You may at least say, "we reject all your proposals, they are gaga, they are rubbish". The then Prime Minister told the two Houses of Parliament in December 1988 the Government will issue identity cards to all voters throughout the country. Now is it permissible to ask whether it is not enough to wait from December 1988, December 1989, December 1990, December 1991 to December 1992?

"Oh it will cost 3,300 crores rupees," they say. "We can't afford it."

But what were you doing sir, since December 1988 when your own Government announced you will give cards?

"Oh, what will you do to *pardanashin* women, they won't get photographed."

We will deal with that.

"How will you deal with that?"

When they apply for a passport they apply a method. I shall use the same method.

For every solution in human existence there is a problem. But let us find the solution by which a fashionable lady doesn't come to my house on the day of the elections and say, "Sir, do you know today I voted six times." Will all the wrongs of the election be defeated by issuing identity cards? You bet they won't be. But at least there will be some little improvement here, some little improvement there.

Coming back the Model Code of Conduct, by the authority of the bench of the Supreme Court the Election

Commission has executive powers. It sometimes partakes of the characteristics of judicial power, sometimes takes after the characteristics of legislative powers. I did not say so, sir. The Supreme Court said so. If what I do is irregular, if what I do is whimsical, if what I do is impertinent, I need to be chopped and sent home as unfit for this purpose. But for God's sake don't throw the baby out with the bath water. The Constitution of India today is standing at a fragile moment and if the methodology of democratic selection of people to represent us continues in the pattern in which it does, at the risk of being grossly misunderstood, I would like to say the time when this country will become a USSR or Yugoslavia is not more than 10 or 15 years away. Because the ordinary man has lost hope that he would get restitution of that which is his rightful due, by rightful methodology. Is it true or not that on hundreds of occasions, little children come and say "I got 90 per cent marks but I couldn't get a seat?" I went to pay my electricity bill today, the bill was Rs. 80, the clerk at the counter said, "unless you give me Rs. 100 I shall not give you the receipt". Once I was at Coimbatore addressing a deemed university of 4,000 college girls. Ten college girls came to me and said, "all ten of us have learnt motor driving. We can do a perfect eight, within the barricades or obstacles erected, in reverse gear. We went to the motor vehicle inspector's office. He said it would cost Rs. 25 for the licence, Rs. 250 for himself. Without that everytime he will fail us." And he has failed them three times. What is the restitution available to these people? When I speak of this, I want to mention that my respect for the judicial institutions of India is unparalleled. I shall not utter a single word. I never did. I never will. Because I have lived and worked under 36 years of the most severe discipline of my own.

Today I have found it necessary to enforce the Model Code, to tell them not to deface other people's property without their approval. The result is that because I am going to Madras, this afternoon my Deputy from Madras rang up to say 150 people are whitewashing the walls in Mylapore relentlessly. I said there are people who are sick, who are tired after a day's work, there are children studying, there are adults doing the work. So don't use mikes from moving vehicles after 7 p.m. and don't use them from static locations after 10 p.m. In every city there is a City Police Act and there is a Commissioner of Police. Yet nobody feels the need to adhere to the laws. Meetings will go on till 10 o'clock, 1 o'clock, 2 o'clock, 3 o'clock. What happens to the poor people living in the surroundings of the place? What happens to the Ministers who relentlessly use government facilities? The Hon'ble Union Minister for Personnel went to Mizoram during the last elections in November using the Defence Ministry's Fixed Wings and helicopters of Indian Air Force to discuss the personnel policies of the Government of India in village after village of Mizoram. And mind you, they are all on certified official duty. The personnel policies of India were determined in the villages of Mizoram because the Minister was there on official work. The Hon'ble Union Minister of Steel was criss-crossing the country in an aircraft belonging to SAIL, to Tata Iron and Steel Company — a private sector company, Indian Iron and Steel Company — a company in pretty grim condition. If the fence eats the crop who will save the crop?

I had a long and running battle with the Government for over one year on what Article 324 (6) of the Constitution said. It states the President and the Government of the State shall on request from the Election Commission make available staff as may be necessary for the conduct of the elections. The Government said, "no, you don't have that power. We will tell you how many policemen you need and you can't ask for more". We had long correspondence on this issue. As the Bible said, *"Before the cock crows twice thou shalt deny me thrice"*. The Cabinet Secretary told me, "No. I have slight differences of opinion on the subject". That matter is pending before their lordships of the Supreme Court. In December, 1988 Parliament passed a law to put two sections: one in the 50 Act and one in the 51 Act, one is called 13 CC and the other number is probably 28 AA or something. And they said the staff connected with the elections shall be deemed as being on deputation to the Election Commission and shall be subjected to the superintendence, control and discipline of the Election Commission. I have with me the speeches made, the statement of objects and reasons with which the Bill was introduced by the Government of that date whose colour was not different from that of today. I have a speech made by the Hon'ble Union Minister of Law Shri Shankaranand and the speech made by the then and now Union Minister of State for Law. In simple monosyllabic words it says, "we want to give the power of punishment to the Election Commission". The right Hon'ble Attorney-General stands in Parliament on 4 August 1993 and says, "we want to make a distinction between discipline and disciplinary procedure". The Attorney-General of India can afford to split hairs, I can't. I hope you won't consider it as a serious offence committed on the propriety of the Attorney-General's statement on the floor of Parliament. I have submitted this to the Supreme Court for a decision. Their lordships have referred it to the Constitution Bench. For me to say anything more would be totally wrong and I shall not open my mouth any more. Whatever decision they hand down, I shall carry it out in letter and in spirit.

We have passed other orders. But I can't take into account the issue of election expenses. The usual explanation of every party's account position is that "this gentleman is my friend, he sent me million posters, he gave me all the *daru*. The third man is also a friend who gave me all the saris for distribution." I can't take it into account and please tell the country that so-and-so candidate distributed 80,000 saris. You can then calculate whether it is Janata Cloth

Scheme sari or something better than that. You can calculate what is the price of a litre of *daru* and how many litres were distributed. I am going to publish them one day. Until Parliament changes the law, I have no power to do anything else with it.

Isn't the present election expenditure limit bad? I have called it a joke. In a formal letter to the Prime Minister I said, "either abolish this joke or change it. But when you change it don't make exceptions". Then I went around with a microscope to scrutinise all the laws and suddenly I came upon Section 171H of the Penal Code which says that if anybody spends money for anybody else without his approval for an election, the man who spends the money can be fined Rs. 500 provided that he can spend ten rupees without prior sanction and then get *ex post facto* approval. It is in today's Indian Penal Code in Section 171H. Look at the extent to which I have gone to find some straw to clutch upon.

There are 24 constituencies which are going to elections on 26 May. We have appointed Commissioners of Income-tax and Collectors of Customs as Expenditure Observers for each constituency. They will go to the press and enquire if this is two-colour poster, how much would it cost, if this is three-colour poster how much does it cost. We go to a constituency and see there are thousands of posters. Do you see the ingenuity of Indians? The other day I was in a Parliamentary constituency. Somebody said the opposite party will deliberately paste a poster in my favour on somebody else's wall and get me into trouble. It happened in Hyderabad. So I said be my eyes, make sure that nobody does this. I think we have a very fertile mind in this country.

I can quote you a thousand judgements of their lordships in courts. On the expenditure point one may quote from one of the most recent judgements of the Supreme Court. The existing law does not measure up to existing realities. The spirit of the provisions suffers from violation through the escape route. The prescription of a ceiling on expenditure by a candidate is an eye-wash. And there is no practical check on election expenses. Even fig leaves cannot hide the reality.

I want to mention to you before closing my random rumblings that the Model Code is not something which I enacted. There is nothing in it which ordinary commonsense would not accept as being something for a fair and even game. You can't find a single clause in the Model Code of Conduct to which any right-thinking person would say, "no no. This was unnecessary". I learn that Parliament is going to make it into a law. Why not? If Parliament makes it into a law, my problem as to whether a particular gesture is a Model Code violation or not would probably disappear. Therefore, my task would be made lighter. People ask me, "who is your master?" I don't know. The Constitution does not tell me. In Section 14 of the Representation of the People Act, it says, "the President shall, on the dates specified by the Election Commission, issue the notification". So does it make me superior to the President of India? Rubbish. I am answerable to the 550 million people of India and in another sense to the 900 million people of India. *"Should I desire to please them I could not then be thine servant"* is what the Bible says.

Today I have an outstanding achievement of being universally hated by all the political parties. It is only a question of degree. If equality of hatred is a test of my impartiality, I will pass with flying colours. This was a country whose heritage was not measured by 25 States and six Union Territories and one Capital Territory. This was not a country of one language. Today, officially this country has 11 languages along with English and Hindi. But in reality it has 4,000 languages. It has 3,000 castes. There are places with 500 inches of rain, there are places with one centimetre of rain. There are places of all kinds of vicissitudes and vagaries. We have learnt to live together a thousand years because like your great grandfather and my great grandfather, I also say

Gangē Cha Yamunē chaiva,
Godavari, Saraswati,
Narmadē, Sindhu, Kaveri,
Jalēsmin Sannidhim Kuru.

An intelligent man once asked me, "where is Saraswati?" So I said, "Go to Prayag". Someone else said, "but Sindhu is no longer in India". Your geography is poor. Sindhu rises in Ladakh and Ladakh is still with us. What was my heritage? Why is it that I should apply *bhasm* on the forehead or put the three-pronged drive on the forehead? No. My religion taught me more than anything else 'tolerance' (*sahishnuta*).

How does one describe one's religion? You have a God like a monkey, you have a God like an elephant, in parts of India, mice are worshipped. But you did not understand my religion or my *virasat*. My *virasat* said when all your questions are over, ask the question *Koham* — who am I? *Kastwam* — who are you?

My *virasat* is not trying to find out whether I am this caste or this subcaste or this subsubcaste? Or is my STD code this or that by which I ring up my God. My STD code was based upon tolerance. And petty pelf politics has converted this country into bit after bit after bit of castes. Into bit after bit after bit of language. I thought the primary purpose of language was to make myself understood to you or for you to make yourself understood to me. It's called communication. When a useless officer today commits the most outrageous mistake, he would cover it up by saying, "Sir, there was a communication gap". This word is an escape route for the majority.

On 14 August, midnight, Panditji stood up on the floor of Parliament and said: "Long years ago we made a tryst with destiny, and now the time comes when we shall redeem our pledge not wholly...but very substantially. ...While the world sleeps, India will awake ...". Panditji, was this the nightmare to which you woke us up?

Is there one square foot of dry ground left in this country where there is no corruption? There is a beautiful word in Hindi and Sanskrit — *brashtachar*. You can't have a more comprehensive word to describe it than the word *brashtachar*. What kind of mockery have we reduced our country to? If I may ask, what is the Lucknow Lawyers' Forum doing about this? Is that question uncomfortable? It's intended to be!

There was a time when somebody became the master of a whole new political weapon, because he was thrown out of a railway compartment. There was a gentleman who was born with silver and gold all over him. He was called to some temple, who chucked off the opportunity and went to jail time after time after time. If you read the panoply of India's great leaders of Independence, 90 per cent of them are lawyers. How many lawyers are there in the panoply of people who are standing up and fighting for that which is right today? And if the answer is uncomfortable, I will give you one lesson. Never invite Seshan for a speech.

I will hold a mirror to your face and if that mirror shows the scars and warts in your face, do not ascribe it to the fact that Seshan is rude. Seshan is a *Khalnayak*. May I ask the Lucknow Lawyers' Forum, in the last five years of its existence how many good causes has it stood for and said that right is right irrespective of consequences? On how many occasions has the Forum stood up and said, "this officer is an honest officer. He is being harassed. Let us back him." I do not want to say so but the backbone of the Executive has been broken by *lalach*, by threat, by harassment. In Italy it was the lawyers and judges who between them found the Mafia and struck at it. Pray, what has the Lucknow Lawyers' Forum done? Did you not find a single civil servant who acted well but was being harassed? Did you stand up to support him? Did you find a single worthless civil servant who needed to be hounded to the ends of the earth? Did you assist in hounding him? If I point an accusing finger, it is not because

I'm notorious for abusing hospitality. That I am. I shall not even ask you for a cup of tea. I shall tell you the truth until it hurts. If reminds me of the big concrete poster of the II Army on the border of Burma within Nagaland which says: "When you go home, tell them of us and say that for their tomorrow we gave our today."

Shall I become Advocate-General? Shall I become ADS to Advocate-General, an Assistant Advocate-General or shall I get a seat on the bench? We have got our own benches. We have crawled our way, and cracked our way and slipped our way to the top and how the mighty have fallen. May I ask, may I beseech, may I beg, may I seek? If there is one community which knows all the onions, it is the lawyers' community. Their lordships on the benches can't do this because they have the restrictions of their seats on the bench. I can't do it because I don't know what the law is.

Election Commissioners will come and go. T.N. Seshan is a *Dhoomketu*. You know what a *Dhoomketu* is? It's a star with a long tail. And to use the language of Omar Khayyam:

> And those who husbanded the Golden Grain,
> And those who flung it to the Winds like Rain,
> Alike to no such aureate Earth are turn'd
> As, buried once, Men want dug up again.

> Think, in this batter'd Caravanserai
> Whose Doorways are alternate Night and Day,
> How Sultan after Sultan with his Pomp
> Abode his Hour or two, and went his way.

> They say the Lion and the Lizard keep
> The Courts where Jamshyd gloried and drank deep:
> And Bahram, that great Hunter — the Wild Ass
> Stamps o'er his Head, and he lies fast asleep.

On 12 December 1996, T.N. Seshan will be comprehensively ex-Chief Election Commissioner. Unless God intervenes at an earlier occasion.

Our country is not made up of individuals. It is made out of a *virasat*. But we probably have failed to keep our *virasat* together. Is our *virasat* in MTV? Is our *virasat* in *Khalnayak*? Is our *virasat* in 'baby' as distinct from you know what else (sexy)? I am a great believer in the Indian movie system. I want to plead with you. I want to beg of you. I want to beg particularly of the lawyers. Please be the conscience of this country. You make the Model Code into a law. Probably, definition is detrimental to the width of applicability. It is like the old principle in physics called the Heisénberg principle of uncertainty, the more you define the more you cannot define. The sum total of definiteness and indefiniteness multiplied together in the laws of physics is the figure which, if I may use my knowledge of physics, is 6.54 x 10 to the power of − 26. That is you put 6.54 and below that you put 1 followed by 26 zeroes. That is the uncertainty. If you try to capture that element more tightly, or the electron or the particle more, it starts exhibiting wave motion. Let me not go into physics.

"You have been painting a picture of pessimism. Why don't you tell us something about optimism?" If I did not possess optimism, do you think, I would still be here? If I did not possess extraordinary optimism to think that if India fails the world will fail, if India survives the world will survive. Not because you and I are Indians and I am a jingoistic. How can this culture ever be allowed to die? So that is a question which I wanted to pose to the Lucknow Lawyers' Forum.

We came to listen to you on Model Code. You talked about everything else except Model Code? If you want a capital 'M' and a capital 'C' and the book printed by the Election Commission, I can send you enough copies, you can read them. But the fundamentality of the Model Code of India is: this country cannot be managed by the laws of engineering except by democracy. You can't run this country by a unitary authority. What are the fundamentals of a democracy? The right to dissent is fundamental to my existence. Equality before law and the rule of law is fundamental to my existence. This man is a VIP and that man is a VOP. A VIP justice and VOP justice by which my father is attacked or my sister is assaulted. The question whether I can file an FIR is dependent upon my relationship with the Daroga. That I venture to say is not democracy. So I repeat after Rabindranath Tagore:

> Where the mind is without fear and the head is held high;
> Where knowledge is free;
> Where the world has been not broken up into fragments by narrow domestic walls;
> Where words come out from the depth of truth;
> Where tireless striving stretches its arms towards perfection;
> Where the clear stream of reason has not lost its way into the dreary desert sand of dead habit;
> Where the mind is lead forward by thee into ever-widening thought and action —
> Into that heaven of freedom, my Father, let my country awake.

If you do this today, in 10 years' time and 15 years' time you will have what the Bhagwad Gita described when Bhagwan showed his *vishwa roop*: If at the middle of the day, a thousand suns should suddenly appear in the sky together, you can imagine the amount of brightness. That is my optimism. My pessimism is, what shall I do with Section 77?

I go from place to place like a missionary asking hundreds of people, "wake up and fight. Build the character of the people of this country. Nothing else will help us, even if you pass thousands of laws."

4

When Knowledge Outstrips Wisdom

For my young friends from the United States particularly, and the citizens of Mysore, let me first introduce myself.

I was born on 15 May 1933, the youngest child of a large family, in a middle class town in Kerala, called Palghat. I am a Palghat Brahmin who represents one of those vicious species of human being which produces four kinds of Brahmins — cooks, crooks, civil servants and musicians. After a very uneventful and somewhat bookworm type of education, I ended up getting a Master's degree in physics from the Madras Christian College in 1952. I taught physics in the same college for three years, from 1952 to 1955. After this brief spell of teaching I joined the Indian Administrative

Speech made to students of Puget Sound University, at Mysore, on 18 February 1994.

Service — India's premier civil service. From 1955 to 1990, slightly under 36 years, I was a civil servant, a permanent civil servant occupying every possible level and I have unusual experiences to my debit. I have run buses, I have done a large number of programmes for rural development. I worked in India's Atomic Energy Programme, in India's Space Programme, in India's Oil Development Programme and more recently I have been Secretary Incharge of Environment, the first civil servant at the top level of Environment and Forests Department, for four years. From the defence of the environment, I moved to the environment of defence. I worked there for a year before I reached the highest level of civil service which is Secretary to the Cabinet. I was a member of the Planning Commission incharge of Science and Technology and Telecommunications and then landed at the present job, much to the misfortune of many men.

That is my brief background. As you would have noticed from my date of birth, I am slightly past 60 and going on 61.

I want to start by telling our foreign colleagues, that India is a country of extraordinary diversity. Geographically it is as diverse as the fact that there is a point in north-east of India — Cherrapunji — where the annual rainfall is 500 inches. It is a different matter that the place has been so denuded of forests that they have acute drinking water problem now. They have cut the trees so relentlessly that all the water that falls there runs off. We have floods and deluges but they have acute drinking water problem throughout the year. They also have a desert in the western part of India, in Rajasthan, where the annual rainfall is less than two inches and it is as good a desert as any desert anywhere in the world. Our vegetation was, if not *is*, as good as in any tropical part of the world. The beauty about India is that from the Himalayan tundras, i.e., the Himalayan ice glaciers where there are miles upon miles of nothing but ice (it is only there that you have the snow leopard, one of the most endangered species in the world today), we have the most diverse tropical forest of the world.

I think there are only two parts in the world where total biodiversity is larger than that which is in India. Those are the Indonesian islands in Central Asia and the Amazonian region. India has an enormous amount of biological diversity. Of this land about 140 million hectares are put to agriculture of which again 30 million hectares are put to agriculture twice a year, so the total annual gross cropped area is about 170 million hectares. About 75 million hectares are said to be forest. I will tell you why I said, "said to be forest" — because not all of this area is covered by trees. Some of them are called forests but they have no growth on them. The balance of other areas goes in lands and buildings and completely inaccessible areas. A few million hectares are under illegal occupation partly by Pakistan and partly by China. I am sure you have been already told that our dispute with Pakistan is questioned. In our dispute with China we are moving towards an agreement and a period of great animus is gently but definitely coming down. They are still occupying some parts of my country.

The population of India in 1947 was 350 million people and as of yesterday morning when I was passing through the biggest hospital in India called the All India Institute of Medical Sciences, in Delhi, where a board announces the growth of population, it showed the figure of 890 million people. Our death rate has fallen steeply during the past 40 years. That happens in every country. We have eradicated tuberculosis. We have largely eradicated malaria, but mosquitoes are coming back with a vengeance because they are becoming immune to DDT. We have got rid of cholera. Consequently, our death rate has fallen sharply and it is in the order of about 18 to 19 per mille. Unfortunately, the birth rate has not gone down equally fast. In all developing countries of the world, if you study, originally both the birth and the death rates are high, and therefore, the net growth rate is small. But then as development takes place, the death rate starts falling suddenly, but the birth rate takes much longer to drop. So in this intermediate period the growth rate goes up. India's growth rate is slightly more than one Australia a year — beyond 15 million people.

You may ask what is India doing about controlling population? I am sure, you must have heard about the way in which the Chinese are controlling the population. We wish them luck. They said nobody can have more than one child. We know what is done to the second child but we don't comment upon it. Our way is our way. Their way is their way. In a democracy, where the rulers have to be back at least once in five years, if not more, to seek votes, we cannot really use stronger methods of controlling population. The only two cases of international success in population control was in Ireland when they faced the potato famine and in Japan during the time of 1945 to 1955 when every single woman in the reproductive age had to undergo five to six abortions per calendar year. They brought down their birth rate to half between 1945 and 1950. Those methods are not necessarily available to us. As such our population growth is one of the biggest problems we face. It is like the chicken and the egg question. How does one control population? Because without control of population, development doesn't take place. The available increases and benefits, whatever the growth rates are, get divided amongst larger and larger numbers of people. So the real growth which you can achieve becomes minuscule sometimes. So what will make the population go down? I am sure your own university and other universities in the US have done regression analysis. After regression analysis you find out that the coefficent which has very positive effect on the decrease of birth rate is infantile mortality.

At the time of Independence our infantile mortality was 300 for every 1000 live births but today it is still a frightening

150 plus per thousand live births. In some parts of India it has gone down to 50 and 40.

We have found several other related factors. Female literacy is one of the most positive coefficients. There are parts of India where female literacy is the highest. If you spend a few days in Kerala, you will find female literacy there is at its highest and the population growth is now down to about 1.8 per cent. Behind female literacy, in a poor country, there is the fact that we have found by regression analysis and actual information that if the girl child has an untorn skirt, that will reduce population rate! Because no girl will go to school with a torn skirt but a boy will go to school with a torn shirt. But there are other factors which help in development, like electricity, the availability of roads to a village, the availability of drinking water, and the availability of a primary health centre where the most elementary diseases can be looked into. Not to speak of complex diseases!

Now the question which arises is — which comes first, development or population control? As far as a democratic country like India is concerned, I am afraid, the only answer is development has to come first. I am sure, you must be doing economics, the famous equation of consumptions plus savings is equal to investment or something else. We cannot save enough. The average saving we do in India is 4 per cent of the gross national product.

I will come back to the way we use the gross national product and savings to which America contributes very largely by arming Pakistan. America has contributed in the last 40 years to our general happiness by giving Leander class frigates to Pakistan for one dollar. They supplied Pakistan F-16s, they have supplied Pakistan Sherman tanks. You're welcome to continue your friendship with Pakistan. We don't look upon these things with anger. We look upon it with happiness. This attitude is part of the Asian culture. Our Independence was backed by Fabian socialism as basis of the thought. When in 1928 the Indian National Congress met in Lahore, the most important speaker at that conference was a gentleman called Jawaharlal Nehru. He laid down that India will follow the path of Fabian socialism. We adopted the path of planned development between roughly 1950 and 1990. It gave us some good results, some bad results. Socialism and planned development were good in parts.

At the turn of Independence in 1947, we had just come out of the fact that British killed three million of my countrymen by a famine in Bengal when they were busy fighting Hitler in Europe and Japan in the East. Three million people died on the streets of Calcutta because of sheer starvation. Again, we hold no anger against the British rule. We still continue to be members of the Commonwealth, we still consider Her Majesty The Queen of England as Head of our Commonwealth. But between 1947, 1965 and 1975, we were beggars begging for food. It was America who supplied us a large quantity of PL-480 wheat. We were a beggarly country importing food right, left and centre and we literally lived from ship to mouth. If the ship did not arrive in Bombay, Cochin or Madras in time, some of us who managed district administration had difficulty in providing wheat to the ration shops. I am mentioning this to tell you where we have changed in the last 20-30 years.

Today we are a gentle exporter of grain. Last year, despite the fact that the monsoon was not satisfactory, we harvested 185 million tonnes of foodgrains. I am not talking of other major crops like cotton and oilseeds and sugarcane. We are also a gentle exporter of dairy products. I think we are the only country in the world which makes *ahimsa* cheese. Anyone who wants cheese made without animal rennet can get it from India.

In 1947, at the time of Independence, the only industrial asset India had was a few textile mills making backing cloth for Manchester to spin cotton into yarn to weave it into the coarsest possible textile. The British used to lease out our forests for building railroads in India and for building ships in Glasgow. So the Indian forest policy was entirely oriented towards supplying timber for the ship-building yards of Glasgow. At that time of Independence we had a small amount of textile work, a small amount of mining work. Other than this, there was hardly any industry. Yes, Tatas built the first steel plant way back in 1918. We learnt the art of making steel but we never learnt the art of making steel plants. Even today, we are a very poor producer of steel.

Between 1947 and now we have progressed enormously in industry. The progress is unbelievable. I still remember when I was working in the Department of Space, when we were making the first Indian satellite, American laboratories used to make fun of Indian national communication satellite by giving it an American acronym and calling it INCEST. I remember going to NASA laboratories in Goddard and seeing in several places cartoon sketches of Indian national satellites. Today, we make our own satellites. We have our own satellites orbiting the earth — our own national satellite of which everything is Indian except the high-quality electronics. It is not worth making a small quantity of that electronic component in this country. We make satellites, rockets, ships, aircrafts and a whole lot of other things.

We certainly have some of the most advanced computing ability in the country. We cannot afford to make computer hardware because the numbers required here are still hopelessly small. But we have parallel array processors with a speed of the best in the world. Over the years our progress has been phenomenal but is it good enough? Has the standard of life gone up? No, it has not gone up. There are social factors which have attracted people into the cities more and more, because the per capita availability of land for those who are engaged in agriculture may be less than half a hectare. If you take a family of five persons the total possession of land they have will not be even one hectare. So the agricultural position is now subcritical. It is not adequate for the purposes of sustaining even one's own family, either in terms of food availability or in terms of economic sustenance or in terms of even employment throughout the year.

When I left the Planning Commission which I left none too soon, the total number of people totally unemployed in the country was 40 million. And there was an enormous amount of disguised underemployment. This number may also be equal to 40 million people or more.

Because of an enormous increase in our population our pyramid is a hopelessly flat pyramid. At the base, the number of children of school-going age is 400 million. Such numbers may frighten you but I cannot help it. This is so because of the enormity of this country. So somebody now might ask, "why don't you reach universal literacy as quickly as possible?" The problem is one of finding resources. An Indian teacher is one of the most poorly paid teachers in the world. The pupil-teacher ratio has become worse between 1947 and 1987. At the time of Independence, the teacher-pupil ratio was one to 40. Today it is one to 80. Our teaching institutions suffer grossly from lack of resources. Unfortunately, our planning has been distorted and we have paid more attention to higher education. In order to satisfy the demands of sunrise industries in California, we produce boys from the Indian Institute of Technology and they promptly go away to the US on whatever visa they can wangle out of the American Consulate. Our best doctors go to the US. This is not a complaint against America. I am only saying that we have an enormous loss of brain power.

The Indian environment, the physical environment, is degrading not at an alarming rate but at an appalling rate. In the ancient days when the population was small, the villagers would go to the forest and do whatever picking ups they could do to find fuel resources. Now the damage done to our forests is not merely due to what local villagers are doing, but the moment you lay a road that road becomes a road for environmental destruction. The average number of trees destroyed in India is ten million per day between sunrise and sunrise. People cut trees ruthlessly — certainly for furniture, certainly for industry, certainly for packing. More than anything else, it is for primary energy. The environment in urban areas is deteriorating at an appalling rate because housing is at such a tremendous premium. Housing is just not available for love or money and people live in pipes. We have water supply schemes for which huge pipes are bought five years in advance. They are allowed to remain on the roads and many people take residence in those pipes. And see pipe dreams inside those pipes.

You will notice one thing at least: that we are not ashamed of our poverty. We are trying to get out of it. But nobody has ever got out of this disease by hiding the fact under the carpet. You have to lay it out in the open.

The amount of freedom of expression my country possesses is unbelievable. Not only for me, I am in an extremely secure position, even people who are not in secure positions can speak the truth about India without fear or favour, without let or hindrance. Whether the President of the United States accepts it or not, I can assure you that for somebody living in this part of the world our human rights are pretty good.

I have told you at the outset that we are a diverse country. How are we diverse, what way are we diverse? From the highest rain to the lowest rain to no rain. From temperatures which in Srinagar go down to minus 50 degrees Celsius at night in December or January to parts of India where temperatures in summer register 50 degrees Celsius. I have told you there are variations of weather, there are variations of temperatures, variations of religions. India has the second largest population of Muslims in the world after Indonesia. India has more Muslims than Pakistan has. Muslims are flesh of our flesh and blood of our own blood. But there are occasions when Hindus and Muslims decide to have a little fun at each other's expense. One Hindu gentleman goes and puts a piece of pork in front of a mosque and all hell breaks loose. A Muslim brother comes and puts a piece of beef in front of one of the temples and all hell breaks loose there also. They kill a number of people and later everything is happily forgotten and we get on to business as usual. We have very ethereal judgements on these things, which are so peculiar that they become very difficult for a non-Oriental mind to appreciate. There is no religion in the world of which a sample is not available in India.

In India we have the worshipping Jains, Buddhists, Sikhs, Christians, Muslims, Hindus. Hindus are not a homogeneous group of people. There are Hindus who think that the only way to propitiate a God or a Goddess is by cutting a neighbour's child. If that is not possible then probably he would cut a goat in order to propitiate his God. There are also Hindus (I am not talking of Jains who do this) who keep a piece of cloth in front of the mouth so that an unsuspecting insect does not go in. For him the idea of non-violence is so all-pervasive. Once I met a saint whom I respected. He was a man who believed so much in non-violence that he would eat nothing that germinates. His entire food used to be a raw banana mixed with yogurt. There are Hindus of all kinds and variations. I do not cast aspersions on Western minds. They have given us good things. We owe to Western civilizations a great deal not to speak of Shakespeare, Wordsworth, Byron, Keats, Shelley and Tennyson. But Western civilization did not understand that Hinduism is not a religion. It is a way of life. You do not understand the distinction between fundamental views — "Oh, you Hindus have funny Gods. I saw a God the other day. It looks like an elephant." What a fantastic joke! The Hindu saw his God in everything living and everything not-so-living. Because the fundamental truth which he learnt in his fundamental philosophies was entirely different. Our Acharyas told us, ask this fundamental question: "What is the purpose of this birth?" Man is only a human being. So man is the only animal who derives knowledge from his ancestors probably much more than animals do. Man is the only animal who can think what the purpose of his life is.

Hinduism does not ask for a particular type of worship. Some philosophers say you have 330 million Gods. So how can this be one religion? An American once wrote that we are an unachieving society because we do not have unequivocal singular views which say this is God. Today you call yourself a Hindu and pray eastwards or you call yourself a Muslim and pray westwards. I am not calling this *Hindutwa*. I am calling it *Bharatatwam* or Indianism. The fundamental of Indianism is tolerance. If you want to find your God facing east, please feel free. If you want to find your God facing west, please feel free. In Hinduism any object you see becomes worthy of worshipping. My grandmother every morning offered a spoonful of milk to a plant. It was her way of saying, thank you God, thank you Nature. The single largest lesson India taught the world is tolerance and today the world is desperately short of tolerance. Everyone today has got an AK-47 or a submachine-gun. And by the time the American lobby decides whether the arms lobby is more powerful than the anti-arms lobby, there will be men who in the morning will get into a small school and kill five or ten children just for the fun of it. I am sorry, I am not looking down upon you. My heart bleeds whether it happens in Washington, New York or Los Angeles.

The fundamental lesson of Hinduism is that you can worship in any way you like. This is the only country where you can say, "I do not believe there is a God". Feel free. You can make your own explanation on whatever happens or does not happen until you reach a point at which you say "probably there is a power greater than all that we have understood".

How do you rationalise many of the practices in Hinduism? How do you rationalise black magic, astrology?

Incidentally I may tell you in addition to various things I am an astrologer also. Why do I believe in all this? Well, if you don't believe it, then you go your way and let me go my way. If you feel your God is in Mecca and Madina, feel free. If you want to say *namaz* five times a day, please feel free. You go to church and read the Bible, feel free. If you want to bombard your own ears with punk rap, feel free. If you want to appreciate Indian classical music, feel free. The fundamental thing of which we have lost sight of is that every man and every woman has a right to live his or her own way so long as he or she does not unnecessarily cross your path. That is the fundamentalism of Hinduism. You won't find it in a million temples. We have got temples in India which show Gods and Goddesses in sexual poses. So what? Every man and woman does have sex. The modern idea is to believe that India has gone prude. India was never prude. It is an open country. Long before blue literature began to be issued in India, *Kamasutra* was written here. It is this variety that is India.

How many languages do we have in India? You take a Rs. 10 or a Rs. 50 note and read its back. You will find eleven languages in addition to English and Hindi. The total number of languages in India is 13. That's the official number. In reality India has several hundred languages.

We have all possible kinds of races: Aryans, Dravidians, Mongols, yellow, brown, deep brown, desperately brown.

There are people who are six-footers or there are people who are three-to-four-footers in height. I am not talking of an odd dwarf in the community.

I venture to tell you, if you want to know India you must know the enormity of its diversity. On this land, one invasion after another took place. History goes back to 300 B.C. when Alexander the Great invaded India. The last to invade India were the Britishers who came in the form of merchants, formed the East India Company and ultimately took over my country due to the folly of my people. We had Chandragupta

Maurya — a great king — who not only ruled what is now India, but also what is Afghanistan today. He went up to Hindu-Kush and beyond. Then came Alexander the Great. Then came X and came Y. Our history is written for us not by ourselves but by the British and who will tell us what is wrong with its history. Notwithstanding their problems, the Britishers gave us the revival of liberal democracy. The Britishers gave us our legal system on the basis of which we today have the Indian Penal Code, the Indian Criminal Procedure Code and the Indian Civil Procedure Code. The British also gave us the railways, the telegraph and they gave us the system of government supported on three pillars. Our system of administration, our system of governance is based on these three pillars — the Executive, the Judiciary and the Legislature. They gave us the English language which is one of the keys to the rest of the world's brain, the rest of the world's capabilities. Today we, of course, want the keys to so many languages — Japanese, Russian, German, French. But the British gave us the keys to the Western languages of the world. I will not inflict any more of my knowledge of history on you because my knowledge of history is highly circumscribed.

But I want to mention to you only one point in passing. And that is, India is the only country in the world which won its Independence entirely by non-violent means. Some of us feel that we got our freedom too easily. Just as someone said "freedom is my birthright", Mahatma Gandhi went to the sea, picked up a handful of ordinary salt and said, "this salt is my birthright". He was not fighting for the salt, he was fighting for fundamental rights of the people. Our greatest weapon was the civil disobedience. The best way of resisting the most wildest dictatorships is through civil disobedience. Gandhiji was put in jail 14 times in India. Pandit Nehru was in jail for a total of 26 years. Even then one must admit that the British gave us a whole lot of good things including the present democratic system. At the same time I want to mention, not because we are jingoistic, that the concept of rule by consent was known to this country 3000 years ago. It meant ups and downs with all types of despots, criminals, crackpots — people who ruled us — which fragmented us into million fragments. The great advantage those days was that there was so little government that an ordinary man couldn't care less who was ruling him.

The post-Second World War Government today is all-pervasive. In India today, if you want electricity, you have go to the Government, if you want cooking gas you have go to the Government, if you want to get into a bus you have go to the Government, if you want a condom you have to go to the Government. The only condom-manufacturing factory in India was a Government factory till a year ago. After Independence in the initial days of enthusiasm we said we shall occupy the commanding heights of the economy. Like many countries of the world, we have now learnt that what is owned by everybody is owned by nobody. It was not merely the World Bank and the IMF who taught us the values of liberalisation. We found it out the hard way. We have found that when the commanding heights of the economy were occupied by a bureaucracy, it led to human reaction which ended up in an economic system which was not based on penalty and rewards, it was not based on merit, it was not based on rewarding hard work, it was based on assured employment. So, therefore, nobody did any work.

I will now tell you about India's elections. India's elections are the eighth wonder of the world. The total number of voters I have on my rolls today is 550 million. That is roughly twice the entire population of the United States. When an election takes place, we set up 800,000 polling booths.

On an average Rs. 2500 million are spent every time we conduct elections in the whole of India. We have raised democracy to such fantastic heights that there are constituencies in which there is not one or two but a 100 candidates. We had one constituency where there were

360 candidates and the ballot paper looked like not just a sheet of newspaper but a full edition of a newspaper. We are stretching democracy to the hilt. There is a very large percentage of people who can't even read the name of the candidate, so each candidate has to be given a symbol. Some party has got a lotus as a symbol, some party has got a hand as a symbol, some party has got a hammer and sickle as a symbol. Somebody has got a wheel, somebody has got a wheel within a wheel. All kinds of symbols are available.

We employ 3.5 million people other than policemen in order to run an election. For a country of this complexity, we have achieved 60 to 70 per cent polling. We have done this, with ten elections to the Lok Sabha — the House of the People. India's voting population is 550 million and the number of seats is 540. And it does not require a mathematical genius to tell you that the average number of voters for a Parliamentary seat is a million people. It is an unbelieveable experience to participate in Indian elections. Nothing like this will you ever see anywhere else in the world.

Today, as the Chief Election Commissioner of India you may ask, "who am I answerable to? I am answerable to the 550 million people.

Whatever the national papers and media may say, my only masters are the people of India. The founding fathers of India's Constitution created the most outstanding of endangered species in human beings called the Chief Election Commissioner. Today I am subject to attacks from all directions because I am going to clean up the graffiti on the wall.

If you open the newspapers you will find all kinds of names by which I am referred to. I am called the mad dog, I am called the mad bull. I am called an Alsatian. In Hindi I have been called a *Khalnayak* which means a villain in the movie. I have been called all kinds of names in the last 12 months. But the game is to clean up the election process. Today, India's elections are watched everywhere in the world.

Yes, our election system is being damaged by various methods and you take your last dollar and bet on it. We have frivolous candidates, bad rolls, rigging, booth-capturing, and all kinds of misdemeanour practices in party elections. Yet, I would like you to go back and tell your friends that India has a demoratic electoral system. There is no electoral system anywhere else in the world of comparable complexity or even half of the comparable complexity. It is such an extraordinary achievement. Despite all the problems, India has one of the freest elections in the world. There is so much freedom that they can write a non-truth and make it appear as absolute truth. I would say that Indian elections are the measure of our strength.

What is democracy? Democracy is rule by consensus. In different translations, Greek would say it is rule by the people and Abraham Lincoln defined it for us in the nineteenth century that democracy is government of the people, for the people, by the people. And today I am telling people we have a democracy in India which is government of some people, for some people, by some people. Ultimately, the world is coming back to one conclusion which is philosophical, which cannot be studied in a political science class, which can't be studied in a specific region, because it is one of the areas where character is going out of the window at the rate of millions of metres per day. If you go to the entire region what is going out very fast is character.

Remember that ultimately for the Indian, the solution is character. It is said that when America sent Armstrong to the moon and set one step for humanity, one Indian gentleman said, "but we will go to the sun". But the assembled group of people said, "but it is very hot there". The immediate reply was, "we would go in the evening". The world is ultimately coming to the conclusion that we are accumulating more knowledge than wisdom. Much bigger and greater people have said this before but let me reiterate it.

India is now rapidly recognising that you can acquire far more knowledge with far less wisdom. You are teaching your children all kinds of technical things — bits and bytes, flips and flops, but you are not teaching your children fundamental ethical values which are not comparable. The fundamental values of human existence are not relative ethics. Example of relative ethics would be whether abortion is a good thing or not, or whether euthanasia is a good thing or a bad thing, you have ethics about whether it is alright to call a black a nigger. These are relative ethics. But the fundamental ethics of truth, compassion and humility have gone out.

What has happened in India is that we have fallen between two stools. We have forgotten our ancient culture. Now we have only the modern culture of rock and rap and crack and smack and heroin. Today we have to decide whether we should crack more because crack has the ability like the Gresham's law of currency, that bad would drive out the good without any effort. Today, like the rest of the world, Indian existence, Indian morality, Indian modes, Indian ethics are getting lost. Is that then alternatively solved by saying that like in ancient India, women should not come out of their house whatever may happen. Is it Indian ethics? I am not the supporter of that. Should a woman pray to God? Why not? The fundamental question is to get back to the question, what is happening to basic human values? The fundamental value of democracy is not the ballot paper or the vote or how much whisky is spilled on the floor of Parliament, or how many mikes you throw at each other in the Assembly in Lucknow. The members had a contest as to who can throw more number of mikes at each other within a given time and a large number of members came out bleeding. They were bleeding for India! That is not democracy. Democracy is a democracy of tolerance.

People think Christianity first came to India with the British. But that's an incorrect piece of information.

St. Thomas, one of the original 25 disciples of Christ, came to Madras in 3 B.C. Even today there is a Basilica of St. Thomas in Madras where he lies buried. Jews came to our country long before the British rule. The fire-worshippers of Ayatollah Khomeini's country came long ago. Today, we are too busy fighting amongst ourselves. That is the basis of our politics. The world at large is watching for an opportunity to plunge on this country to tear it apart. And we are sometimes not aware of this danger. I hope some day we would realise it and clean up our country.

I would summarise by saying, ours is a country of enormous diversity. It is a country of enormous history. Here is a country of human thought. Anyone who wants to specialise in India should learn Sanskrit. There is no grammar, according to computer experts, as comparably good as Sanskrit grammar for computerisation. I am not saying this because I am a jingo. There are million things wrong with us. But what is fundamental of this country is its past, which makes me ask the 2500-year-old fundamental question: Who am I? Is there an answer? Is it only the body? No. Is it the sense with which the body is affected — the eyes, the nose, the ears, the tongue, the skin? No. Is it the mind? Is it the intellect? Is it the habit of being conscious and opening up? Is there an 'I' which is more fundamental than that which says "who am I?"

Then my philosophy also taught me to ask the question "who are you?" Are you different from me? When an average Indian presses his hands and says *namaste* he is not saying "good morning". *Namaste* means I bow to you. What do I bow to — your shirt, your face, your hair? No. I am reverentiating that which is inside you. Which is no different from that which is inside me which is the fundamental truth. *Ekam satyam*. The truth is one and the learned speak of it in many ways. You teach the world unequivocal, unitary values of protestant ethics. I have no complaint. I am a great student of the Bible. And I am willing to say that it is better to light one candle from the original light than curse the darkness. No religion taught any group of people to be intolerant towards the rest of the people. The fundamental evil in the world today is that knowledge is outstripping wisdom.

5

"Rishvateva Jayate"

It is my conviction, whether you accept it or not, that until and unless we rectify this decayed, damaged, dilapidated empire called Indian democracy all that you may do, whether it is for milk or it is for oil, is paint a picture on water.

It is a misfortune of the existing generation that most people have no concept of what India is all about when they speak about India. And would you permit me to spend a few minutes telling you about that which is India. India comprises 25 States, six Union Territories and a National Capital Territory of Delhi. India is a country of party A, party B, party C, party D with assorted parties thrown in at the States. Today they teach the young people of this country the history of India in bad English and say Ashoka 'dugged' wells and

Speech made at the National Dairy Development Board, Anand, on 7 March 1994.

'builded' hospitals. Is that Indian history? They have tried to make us learn and say that the Chalukyas fought with somebody else and the Kakatiyas fought someone else and Cheras and Cholas fought with somebody else. Is that history? I venture to submit to you that is not Indian history. The British wrote the history of India for us, which made us wonder whether India was a country worthy of its name. A country with 33 crore Gods. What kind of religion is it? In my religion there is only one God. This India you talk about is a woman of extraordinary diversity. Why a woman, why not a man? Because no man is capable of this amount of diversity. How many languages are there in India? Today, according to the Government, we have a total of 13 or 15 languages. No Sir. India has got 800 languages and scripts. Mark my word for it. This comes from the Central Institute of Indian Languages, Hyderabad. Not all of them have scripts. Not all of them have large numbers who speak it. Even when you talk about Hindi, Hindi is not a unitary language. This Hindi you talk about is not a single Hindi — you have Bhojpuri, you have Vaishali, you have Maithali, all kinds of Hindis all together pass for Hindi.

How many religions are there in India? Where is a religion in the world which is not available in India? Certainly there is Hinduism, there is Islam, there is Christianity, there is Sikhism, Jainism, Buddhism. Jews are available in this country, Parsis are available in this country, animists are available in this country. My religion was not based upon idols and symbols. It was based upon a far more fundamental truth which long ago, 3000 years ago, when you were still living in caves, my forefathers taught me the fundamental of truth and said truth is so difficult to define. As the Vedas said: it is not this, it is not that. Ultimate truth can be defined only by this negation. Is Hinduism a single-point religion? Equivocal? No. You are free to find your God the way you choose to. You can find your God standing on a single leg in front of the Varanasi river. You find it by killing a goat, dropping its blood in front of Kali. You find it by sitting in front of a river for months and years together observing total silence. All of this and much more *was* Hinduism. Because my Hinduism did not teach me to go and drive a knife into somebody or set fire to his *mohalla*. The ultimate centrality of truth is consciousness. Not the consciousness of somebody who is not awake, asleep or gone into a spell or fallen unconscious. But there is consciousness central to the existence which my ancestors said in term of *Pragnanam Brahma*. That is the fundamental which I learnt. I did not see my God merely in this or that. You thought my Rangoli was God. You thought my picture was God. You thought my three-dimensional sculpture was God. No, none of these was my God. "Then why do you worship this?" As somebody answered years ago, "if I kick your photograph won't you become angry? I am not kicking you, I am only kicking a piece of cardboard and a piece of photographic print. Why do you get angry?" I am not here on a philosophic trip. All I am going to tell you is that I don't call my religion Hinduism. I venture to tell you that if more lately you might have decided that your God is in Mecca or Madina or in Bethlehem, it makes no difference to me. It does not matter to me whether you find your God in seven, eight, six or you find your God in saying RIP. Because in each of these religions there are subreligions and subcastes. There are 4000 castes in this country. How many castes does Hinduism have? Has anyone ventured to list the number of castes in Hinduism? Do you know this story? In Madras some years ago they went and starved an elephant to death trying to decide whether it was Vadakale or Tenkale. The only difference between these two is, one kind puts a white chalk piece outside and a red piece inside without a tail. And the other kind puts a tail on that white chalk. In deciding whether the elephant belongs to this chalk or that chalk, they killed the elephant by starvation.

My Hinduism is not a Hinduism which restricts. I call my Hinduism *Bharatatwam*. What this country taught the world was *Sahishnuta*: tolerance. And today the world is desperately short of that one commodity. You talk of the great American dream: 16 kinds of milks, 60 kinds of chocolates, 16,000 kinds of cars. "Are you jealous of it?" No. Jealousy is something which you do not have at the age of 60, when you have silver in the hair. I do not even have silver in the hair, I have *Sahara* in the hair, gold in the tooth, lead in the legs. I am not talking of envy or jealousy, yet anybody can go and pick up a machine-gun, walk into a school and kill 20 children for no reason at all. Because probably he has fought with his wife or he came out of a distorted family of husband and wife in perpetual quarrel. It is better to belong to a single parent family than to be a child in a family where there is distorted relationship between the husband and the wife. Likewise in India somebody superimposed his views and said "women cannot read Vedas". It is convenient to create some rubbish by saying that women cannot read the Vedas. Where is it written that women cannot read the Vedas?

There are only four blood groups, with two variations. There is A, there is B, there is AB and O, and there is RH positive and RH negative. When you say this you have described all the possible varieties of human blood. Then who is this trying to tell me, "You are Yadav, I am OBC, I am BBC, and CBC". Kerala and neighbouring states are fighting over whose cashewnut it is. In Karnataka and Tamil Nadu, they are trying to find out whose river Cauvery is. Cauvery has the dirtiest bit of water and still my grandmother said, "please bring all the waters into this country". We have lost Sindhu to the Zulfiqars and Benazirs long ago. How many ways in which can you wear a single piece of six yards of textile around the body of a beautiful woman? It becomes fashionable for South Indian children to walk around in the Gujarati way of wearing a sari. Then you have a Coorgi way of wearing a sari, you have the Bengali way of wearing a sari of which the fundamental is that the bunch of keys must be at the end of the sari, so that the daughter-in-law will not take it away from you. What have we not done to split this country into little bits and pieces in the name of water, in the name of language and in the name of religion?

Today India is backward, India is hungry, 25 per cent of the people are living in slums. Bombay's population has crossed ten million. Fifty per cent of it is living in *jhuggis* or *joparpattis*. Delhi is inching towards ten million out of which 45 per cent is living in slums, brought in by some outstanding political leaders. Shall I mention you the name? Why should I?

This India of mine, this India of yours, this India of ours was a great country long before the Britisher had found his spinning-jenny through which we made cloth. Long before that we used to make textiles which ran through a ring in order to make the world's most beautiful muslin. India exported all kinds of spices to the West. It exported knowledge. What is this Arabic numeral? The Arabs took it from us during the course of trade, sent it to the West and the West today calls it the Arabic numeral. That is why the Indian Constitution (one of the world's most secular constitutions) says that when Hindi is used as an official language the numeral to be used is the international form of the Indian numeral. Why should they be so apologetic about it?

Today all our linguistic harlots must put the bus number, bus route number only in Devnagri numerals. They must have car plate numbers in Devnagri because they forget that the fundamental purpose of language is communication. Does anybody sit back to ask the question, "what is the purpose of language?" Is it to divide? Is it to prevent somebody talking to somebody? We have an apocryphal story of a Sardarji who was asked by a Tamilian: '*Tamil teri ma*'? (which when translated meant whether the Sardarji knew Tamil). The Punjabi got very angry and replied: '*Punjabi tera bap*'. What fantastic improvements have we made in education since Independence! A country which had 13 universities, today has more than 200 universities. There are specialised universities like agricultural universities, horticultural universities, animal husbandry universities. There are central universities, there are affiliated universities, there are deemed universities, there are undeemed universities, there are universities without Vice-Chancellors and Vice-Chancellors without universities. In Tamil Nadu we have a university, which has had no Vice-Chancellor for the last six months. In Kerala, they have a university where a Vice-Chancellor cannot enter, because the students said "we have had enough of you, do not come in". And yet the state of education in this country is such that it needs one order of the Supreme Court a day to regulate medical college admissions. What price education?

Can one stop talking about the diversity of this country? Just think of the variety in dresses. Just a plain *dhoti* can be worn in 18 different ways. The Andhra way of wearing it, the Tamilian way of wearing it, the Kerala way of wearing it, the Gujarati way of wearing it, the Maharashtra way of wearing it, the Bengali way of wearing it. The reason I am mentioning to you about the diversity of this country is that somebody does not say, "isn't it time to have dictatorship?" No way. Our country can't have dictatorship. The country in its wisdom showed in 1977, as most people were afraid of saying in 1975, that "we don't want dictatorship". We would much rather breathe the free air rather than get the benefits of somebody putting up a poster at Delhi airport saying 'Progress is a one-way street, keep moving' — which was done in 1975. Keep moving into the Muslim parts of the country with bull-dozers?

I don't want you to get into doubt at all whether we can govern ourselves by any methods other than democracy because if there are two Indians there will be a minimum of three opinions. So how can these people be governed by one man's opinion? It is like 'keep to the left' rule which a Commissioner of Police is trying to enforce in the streets of

Anand. And no one believes in keeping to the left. This country cannot be governed except by democracy.

Democracy's pillars are the right to dissent, the right to justice. There can't be one law for somebody and another law for somebody else. You will ask, "then how come the laws change with the VIPs"? India always had equality before the law. There was a king in Chola who had hung a bell and said anybody who is dissatisfied with justice can come and ring it. And one day the king was sitting in the courtyard when he heard the bell. He came out and found that a cow was ringing it. Since the king had the ability to talk to cows, he asked, "what ails thee?" The cow said "your chariot ran over my calf and killed it". Whereupon the king said, "cut my head". And his head was cut off. Today the VIPs do not know how to talk to human beings, leave alone cows and calves.

But this country will not survive as one country if this kind of democracy carries on. A MARG poll says 58 per cent of the country is in favour of dictatorship. "It is now very clear that what we need is a benign dictator". But where shall we buy him? Is he available in Connaught Place? Is he available in Flora Fountain? Is he available on Mount Road? Is he available in Chowringhee? We cannot get a benign dictator. Any person who becomes a dictator becomes malignant in 24 hours. There is an English saying, power corrupts, absolute power corrupts, absolutely. Somebody corrected me the other day and said "power *tends* to corrupt, and absolute power *tends* to corrupt absolutely".

There is a law in this country for *every* purpose. I am told by some judges of the Supreme Court that the *per capita* availability of laws in the world is nowhere as high as it is in India. And implementation of them is nowhere as deficient as in India. But, none of these gets implemented and the rest of the population of the country lives happily ever after. India has the world's best Constitution taken out from the unwritten Constitution of Britain, American Constitution, the

French Constitution, the German Constitution. Every Constitution put together is the Constitution of India. You have added one more schedule about defection. There is one more law which says twenty divided by three is not less than seven. Does it sound familiar? Twenty divided by three is not less than seven suitcases perhaps.

The Constitution of India, the like of which the rest of the world has not seen, was amended 73 times in the course of the last 45 years. The 73rd amendment was passed recently. I suspect that today's newspaper says it is going to be amended for the 74th time in order to clip my wings because I am a bird. One day the Government realised somebody can misuse the Constitution. So somebody went and passed a law saying that the President can return a proposal of the Cabinet once. After the nightmare of 1975 to 1977, the Constitution was amended to say that the President cannot say no to a signature, if it is sent back to him once again by the Cabinet. "Oh, Seshan why do you bother about these Rajya Sabha members and their ordinarily residence status"? I said, "What wrong have I done?" "Seshan tries to find a new law." What rubbish. The law says nobody can be a candidate for the Rajya Sabha unless he is 35 years of age, he is of sound mind, etc., and an elector in that State. Today they are talking of amending the Constitution to take this law away. I have no problem. Whatever rule the Federation of Football Associations lays down, I will blow the whistle according to that rule. But do not blame me for blowing the whistle according to *your* rules. I am *not* saying this is my rule. How many of you have read the Constitution of India of which the first Article does not say that India will be divided into states. It said India shall be a Union of States. Which came first, the hen or the egg?

The Rajya Sabha alone has got extraordinary powers. May I give you the simplest of examples? If the Rajya Sabha passes a resolution, and says this subject is transferred from the State list to the Union list, it is valid for one year. If the

Lok Sabha passes it, that change is not valid. The Rajya Sabha is the only Sabha which has the competence to pass a resolution saying prohibition would be taken out of the State list and put into the concurrent list or the Union list. Only the Rajya Sabha can pass it. That is why the founding fathers passed a law and said that Rajya Sabha members are the representatives of the States. And how do you find they are representatives of the State? They must be electors in the State. Somewhere else they wrote in the 1950 Representation of the People Act, in order to be a representative, one should be an elector and in order to be an elector he should be 21 years of age. No, now we have progressed with the rest of the world, so we made it 18 years of age. You should not be of unsound mind, you must not be disqualified under any law in force and you must be an ordinarily resident there. And you go and say I am ordinarily a resident in the outhouse of the *sarpanch* of the village, where there is no piece of furniture, where there is not even a three-leg stool. If the honourable Foreign Minister of India is elected from some village of Haryana he is an ordinarily resident because he has taken the outhouse of the *sarpanch* on rent though he has not stayed there even for one day since he registered himself — neither before nor after. They said: "Manmohan Singh is a good Minister. Why are you after him?" So good Ministers are exempted from the requirements of the law? Long before I even dreamt of coming into this chair, Manmohan Singh was my benefactor par excellence. He used to treat me like a younger brother, or even a son, with such tender affection. I am only trying to say that there is one law. That law must be enforced on everybody, without fear or favour.

There are the Parliament and the State Legislatures to make laws. What kind of Parliament do we have? Would it be wrong to say that a vote of confidence is passed on the floor of Parliament by imported liquor? Didn't we see somebody vomiting imported liquor and pressing the wrong button when the vote of confidence was taken on the floor of the Lok Sabha on 28 August 1993? Or, is it that those who are doing wrong things are not doing wrong but those who speak about it are wrong people? In 1991, I had 200 election deaths during the elections in UP. In November 1993 there were two deaths on an election day in Itah and they were not connected with the elections. But since they took place on an election day they said 'election murders — 2'. And yet at the end of it our friends in newspapers tell me that out of 425 members in UP Assembly, about 180 have criminal records. Of these one member has 18 FIRs — not one or two but 18 FIRs for murder against him.

There is a Legislature and then there is a Judiciary and there is an Exeuctive.

What a stage this country has passed to in terms of its Executive! Was this the country which produced H.M. Patel? Was this the country which produced Chintaman Deshmukh? I keep saying that the Indian Civil Service was neither Indian nor civil nor service. What is the Indian Administrative Service, except saying: I Am Sorry. I am saying in public that the civil service in India has got reduced to the condition of polished call girls. Several people wrote to ask me, "what is your experience with call girls?" How does it bother you? It is like the lady who went to the zoo and went on asking the zoo-keeper the age of the hippopotamus. And he went on saying "Madam, I do not know." And the lady was also looking something like a hippopotamus. Finally, the zoo-keeper lost his temper and said, "Madam, the only person who can have an interest in the age of a hippopotamus is a hippopotamus of the opposite sex, are you that?" What does it matter what my experience with call girls is? Have you not converted the civil service of this country into a hopeless pulp? It is nice to criticise and say they do not stand up. Who reduced them to this condition? The politicians? No. You did it. I accuse you. When a good civil servant was there, nobody stood up to support him. When a bad civil servant was there,

there was hardly anybody who stood up to say, "this fellow is a rascal, throw him out." Is it not true? The younger generation, the largest number of them who are between the age 20 and 30 are not more responsible. But I am talking of the old people, what were they doing when this was being done? Of course when the officers found confrontation not very successful, they become collusionists, and they are fully committed to it. Why not? If the house is on fire, why not go in and pick up at least a fountain pen lying on the table.

The government of this country is described as 10 per cent government or 15 per cent government, in different parts of the country. "If I am getting 10 per cent for somebody, why not retain 1 per cent for myself." But at the bottom of all this corruption is election. When I finish the analysis of the three gigantic pillars of India's democray — the Legislature, the Judiciary and the Executive — you and I can for the rest of the evening, rest of the week, rest of the month, rest of the year, rest of our lifetime, exchange stories as to who was more corrupt than who.

In this connection I turn my attention to the media. In any case, it will write something against me, so how does it matter, whether the water goes over the head one foot or 1000 feet? The result is the same. What have the journalists of India done? Their contribution is limited to say that this man is right and that man is wrong. I won't say more except asking you to show me one square foot of dry ground in this entire country. You are trying to paint on a canvas which is fraying. In the middle it is tearing. Where is it tearing? It is tearing in the Punjab, it is tearing in Kashmir, it is tearing between Assam and Nagaland, it is tearing in Bihar, it is tearing in the Naxalite regions of Gadchiroli. It is tearing in Bastar, it is tearing in Raipur, it is tearing in Hyderabad and Vijayawada, it is tearing in Tamil Nadu, Kerala, it is tearing in places in Maharashtra where RDX has landed. All over the place, this canvas is being torn apart by people who are sitting at the top of the branch and cutting the bottom. And mind you, I am not talking about India, democracy and elections, but about sweat, toil and tears.

Someone asked me the other day, "Sir, are you for Narmada or against Narmada?" I am neither pro-Narmada nor anti-Narmada. But tell me some method to produce grain? Every day the number of trees cut on an average is one crore. As Mary Antoinette was telling people to eat cakes when bread was not available, several people here say 'give them gas'. As if anything else is being provided by the entire public sector of this country except gas of different types, not just the cooking variety.

A country which could not produce enough grain to meet its requirement, today is making enough grains, so that the Agriculture Ministry can gently say, "may we export at least Basmati rice? Let us also export cotton, long staple cotton." For three months they allow exports. And when my friends have finished the export they clamp restrictions on export again. This is a typical scenario.

The country did not produce enough milk, but today we are a country suffering, at least in the marketing sense of the word, from the problem of surplus milk. Dr. Kurien is just back having visited China to offload some milk on the Chinese. Today milk is flowing in India; never mind, if the milk sometimes turns rancid. I won't elaborate on that because why talk of coal in Newcastle. There was a time when India could only produce the coarsest variety of textile to supply the Birmingham industry. Today we wear all kinds of apparel chiefly produced in India. Today even our policemen are clothed in terylene. I think that is quite an achievement!

A country which did not make pins and needles is today making planes, rockets and satellites, and we do have computers and biotechnology and God knows what else.

On the surface level one can go on quoting our success story but on the inside there is room for appalling fear because what passes for the central control of this country is in its ruling institutions. And what passes for the ruling institutions of this country is not even a parody but it is a calamity on all that is truth, justice and equity.

I want to come back to the rhetoric in favour of all the fantastic improvements we have accomplished. At Independence, the average life expectancy was 36, and today it is 57 for men and 58 for women. There is in-built strength in women which can only be described by the word *Shakti*. In our national eradication programmes, you put the word 'national' and in between you put any word, be it malaria, falaria, salaria. Everything is eradicated. In all our crash programmes, everything has crashed. That is why they are called 'crashed' programmes. At the end of all these programmes what is the quality of life in Haryana? Literacy amongst women as of last year was 5 or 10 per cent. In Bihar, it was less than 10 per cent. Yes, in Kerala the literacy rate among women is 70 or 80 per cent. It is not because of you and I; it is because the society of Jesus and Christians found out that the best way to the heart of a human being was through his stomach, through his illness, and through his children. They looked after the children, they looked after their health. Gentlemen sitting in the Bhavans of Delhi take the credit for what the padre did 75 years ago. Somebody may get angry at these remarks of mine because I was also part of the Planning Commission once upon a time!

So what is the quality of life in this country? Will you agree with me that the ultimate basic requirement of a human being is *roti, kapda aur makān*? And so many people in the country live in *jhuggis* and *jhoparpattis*.

What are the characteristics of a city? It must have accommodation, it must have power supply, streets, drinking water, sewage. It must have local transport and local community requirement within the community. Which city in India passes this test? Imagine there are parts of Delhi — the capital of the country — where there is no electricity most of the time, there is no water most of the time, there is no housing most of the time. Somebody was telling me the other day in Maharashtra the Government had built houses for slum-dwellers. But executive engineers of the Government are staying in those slum improvement houses. They are built by the munificence of a hundred crores of rupees to Bombay. I will tell you my favourite joke. In all the cities of this country there is no power shedding because power shedding does not take place in India. That is load shedding. Nobody sheds power. It is a characteristic of power that once you acquire it either by election or by appointment, you never shed it. One of the fundamental laws of Indian thermodynamics is that you never shed power, you only shed load. I am only trying to suggest that the quality of life in this country has reached abhorrent levels. What will Dunkel do to us, what will Dunkel do to drinks, what will Dunkel do to milk? Are you going to patent seeds in this country? What a tragedy it would be, if you patent seeds. I take no sides. Dunkel is of no concern to me.

There was an Air India hoarding during the Kerala elections 25 years ago. "Kerala elections", Air India wrote, "is nun of my business". Because nuns were being exported in large numbers. I want to tell you the quality of life in this country is atrocious but that alone does not bother me. What ultimately bothers me is that every single institution of this country is eroded and centrally eroded by corruption. I have suggested and I make the suggestion once again for my Gujarati friends. For your benefit each one of you rub off that statement which says below the three lions *Satyameva Jayate* and change it to *Rishvateva Jayate*. What else will be more appropriate?

Tell me one aspect of life in this country which is not steeped in corruption. You may well ask, "how does it concern you, Sir, why don't you talk about elections?"

Yes, it concerns me. Because the fundamental of corruption in this country is the election. It is based entirely on cash, corruption and criminality. People ask me, "Sir, what is wrong with India's elections? Why don't you tell us." Usually

I answer it with "what is right with India's elections?" There are people who go Yajur Veda, Sama Veda and Atharva Veda but primarily most elections are done on the basis of Rig Veda. Because they are often based on rigging and booth-capturing. And this because the civil service in India is a committed civil service now. Don't think I am only talking of the IAS. I am talking of the highest man in the highest chair in Delhi to the lowest man in the lowest *mohalla* in the village. They have decided that it is better not to swim against the current. But along with the current you can pick up whatever you can pick up *en route*. Whom do you hold responsible for all this? The civil service and its neutrality is the central kingpin on which the entire election system rests.

In Tripura I caught the IG of Police, the DIG of Police and the Collector sitting with a party Minister and party workers, discussing how to capture votes. But I couldn't do anything. Because the government says, "you don't have the power". "How did the UP elections pass off peacefully in November?" I've my suspicion that it has something to do with the business equipment carried. As many as 60,000 men were sent to UP and that had its effect. There was the highest voter turn-out and hundreds of poor people came and said, "in all our life this happens to be the first time that we could vote". Why was everything quiet and silent? Because business equipment was available. The Bible says: "The fear of the Lord is the beginning of Wisdom".

I have been repeatedly asked why I postponed Punjab elections at the last minute. Well, let me tell you, because when I sent 39 Joint Secretaries to 13 Parliamentary constituencies all 39 of them wrote, "it is a mad man who will run an election in Punjab at this juncture." His Excellency General O.P. Malhotra, the Governor of Punjab, met me and said, "I want a postponement". He then went to the Secretariat and had a meeting with the Prime Minister. He came back and told me, "No, no I don't want any postponement". In two hours there was a sea-change. So I said, "what has happened in Punjab, have they produced a hundred Gills or what?" He said, "No no, it is our own decision." Then I wrote to the Home Secretary to the Government of India: "About 125 people have been pulled out of trains and killed in cold blood in the last 48 hours. The car of the Honourable Minister of State for Home Subodh Kant Sahay has been blasted by a mine. You think Punjab is in a fit condition?" I got a reply from the Home Secretary to the Government of India saying, "we have sent 10 more companies". What kind of companies have you sent? What is the number of people in ten companies, I don't know. I only asked him whether the law and order situation in Punjab is appropriate for holding an election or not. I will tell you more of it on 12 December 1996 — the day I retire.

During the last July elections I had asked the Government to send more police to Tamil Nadu because the Chief Minister was being rather strong. About 20 Congress MPs said that "we can't even go to the villages because they beat us up with cycle chains." So I said, "please send some Central police". The Chief Minister asked for seven companies and they gave her seven companies of Central police. They could have left it at that. But the Government of India gratuitously decided to add to the insult and said, "you have no right to ask". Whereupon I postponed the elections till December. All hell broke loose in Parliament and the right honourable Attorney-General came and expressed his right honourable views. The Government said, "we will take it to the Supreme Court". I waited for 48 hours. They did not. Hence I took it to the Supreme Court at 10.45 A.M. At 4.40 P.M. the Chief Justice of India said, "the powers are with you" and I pulled the elections back. So what mistake did I make? I am not, as you seem to imagine, a piece of footmat for you to rub your dirty leg every time you come in and go out.

Let me come back to the question that the central basis of democracy in India is the three pillars of cash. Cash requires corruption before, during and after. And corruption requires criminality. The criminals first served other people and then they said, "why should I serve you, I will do it myself. I myself will go to the Assembly or Parliament." The result is before you.

The centrality of Indian politics today is cash, criminality and corruption. Who is responsible for this? I say, with great humility, you are responsible. This country sat and watched every single thing that was central to our existence being destroyed by repeated blows on the body politic and everybody kept quiet saying that this doesn't concern him. "We don't go to the polling booth. We don't vote, we don't have a vote." Or "I had a vote, but by the time I went there somebody else had voted." Or "I went to the polling booth, they said 'you are all right, your age is all right, address is all right but in my polling list it says you are a woman'."

Everybody is angry with me, I get hundreds of letters per day with the question, "why is my name not in the list?" Am I supposed to check 550 million names? Even if I were God personified I could not have checked it up. There is a conspiracy of both inefficiency and deliberate deletion of names in the polling lists. Today spreading from the origins of Rig Veda in West Bengal and in other States names are being deliberately deleted. There are many people who come and say their outhouse servant's name is in the list but their own names are not there and this is very socialistically done. Names excluded in Delhi included such 'minor' names as Vishwanath Pratap Singh and Chandrasekhar. They are not in the list, they are not yet 18!!

In February 1992 at the Prime Minister's request I had put all the electoral reforms into one piece of paper and sent it to him. And in that I told him: Your Government promised to give identity cards. Please don't make it just an election card, make it a multipurpose card. So that people will jump over each other to get the cards. Make the card useful for ration, make the card useful for employment, make the card useful for hospital, school and everything." From February 1992 to August 1993, I waited and waited. In reply there was a thundering silence. Finally in August I got into action since I have the powers to issue the order. Whatever I can cure, I will cure. I have found out 150 ways in which elections today are being damaged. I would like to publish them one day for the country to know about it.

Somebody had asked the Chinese, "in which directions are your missiles aimed at?" The Chinese technician, who did not wait for the reply from Beijing, said, "the aim is at all 360 degrees". Likewise I am trying to deal with problems related to every part of the election. There are some which are within my powers. You bet your last penny that if it becomes necessary I shall grunt, I shall growl, I shall bark and ultimately I shall bite. And don't ask me why an *Alseshan* bites because it is customary for an *Alseshan* to bite. For, it is better to light one candle than to curse the darkness. Hence light one candle. Next time there is an election and somebody who is not fit stands for election prevent him. Stop wrong people from trying to get into the Assemblies and Parliament. You can. Tell your children, sisters and brothers not to burn buses because the only person to profit by burning buses is the glass company and the purchase manager of the transport system. Because he gets his 10 per cent. Whose buses are you burning? These are my buses and your buses. It is my train and your train that you are burning and throughout the country the poor young children have been made pawns in this game of chess.

My objective is to hold a mirror to you and say, "I accuse you". Because when your mother and my mother were being subjected to harassment you kept silent. My generation is about to slip out of active work. For God's sake get up and fight.

The media thinks I am angry. I am not capable of being angry. I am angry only on behalf of this country. Is this the country of Gurudev Tagore who wrote: "Into the Heaven of Freedom let my country awake"? What kind of Heaven are you waking up into? And on 26 January, you will all sing 'ham bulbulen hain iski'. *Kiski bulbulen hain?* Have you ever seen a single person in India who wants to say that "I want to stand for elections, but I will not accept any job." Have you seen such a character in this country? Probably they existed in the 50s. Isn't that the travesty of human justice that the entire lot of the country's politicians today are full-time professional politicians?

Please find a better government for this country, please find better representatives for this country. If you can improve the system one little bit, please do it. As far as I am concerned I am Bhishma lying on a bed of arrows. I will go when *Uttarayan* comes. And my *Uttarayan* comes when there are enough of you making noise. I will give you one assurance which you can quote: if I am not able to wake up the people of this country, in the next few months, I will get up and quit. I give you an absolute assurance that I will not quit out of fear. That is an absolute hundred per cent assurance. But I fear, I might come to the conclusion that this is an unawakable propensity, there is no point in trying to wake it up and for God's sake don't make me go home compulsorily.

Throughout the length and breadth of this country nobody is willing to accept his responsibility, whether he is civil or he is uncivil. If you don't take some civil methods of cleaning up this country, I assure you either this country will break up into Bosnia or Herzgovina and Sarajevo or Armenia or evil forces will take over in unitary authority where freedom will become a non-entity. I want to mention this to you with humility, I want to mention this to you with agony, not with anger, not with a set objective of my own in mind, please for God's sake get up before it is too late. This is the same song I sing everywhere and I have sung the song in front of you also.

6

History is Good for Lunch, Not for Sleep

Years ago, our forefathers made a tryst with destiny. We have made fantastic amount of progress since then. We have enormous amount of modern information technology related to the computer, computer software, and computer hardware. We are way up somewhere near the top of biotechnology, not quite at the top though. And some of the world's most difficult algorithms are solved by Indians educated in IITs of Delhi, Bombay, Calcutta, Madras and Kharagpur. We have several successes to our credit, all of which it is not my intention to list. I used to live as an anonymous quill-driver, in the days in which these progresses were made in the field

---

Speech delivered for the Citizens for National Consensus, Bombay on 20 December, 1993.

by the governments at the Centre and in the States. Yet in a large part of this country today there is no drinking water. It may be six and a half years from now, in the middle of year 2000, the population of India will cross a billion mark, that is, a hundred crore of people. But would you believe me, when I tell you that out of those, 40 per cent, 400 million people, larger than the rest of the world put together, will be living in urban agglomeration areas by 1 July A.D. 2000 which is not very far away. God willing, God unwilling, many of us will still be around at that time. Out of these 400 million people, at least 50 per cent, if not more, will be living in slums. You can give these clusters various names. You can call them *jhuggies*, you can call them *jhoparpattis*. Only the pronunciation will vary.

Yes, we are all willing to pat ourselves on the back and say that much of the literacy which is now available is because of the National Literacy Mission. Where have you succeeded most? You have succeeded in Kerala. But for God's sake Kerala got literacy not because of the National Literacy Mission but because of the Christian missionaries, who came in for their own purposes and decided that education and health are the best ways to make inroads into the human mind. I can go on describing the State that is India, and paint a rosy picture. Bombay is one such city where it takes you one hour to cross Churchgate. Fantastic improvement in the last five years, since I left Bombay. Another five years, you will stop all stops at Churchgate for we will need a large amount of bread to dispose of the jam. As Sanjay Gandhi said, "progress is a one-way street, keep moving". We are not even able to keep moving.

It is very pleasant to hear nice things about oneself. But how does an average Indian, a child of 20 or 22, 23 or 25, look upon India. It is less than a few months ago that we celebrated the Golden Jubilee of the Quit India Movement. I think the children of India have adopted another Quit India Movement. Not the same as was adopted on the sands of

Chowpathy. The best children now are fond of Texas, or Florida, or Miami, or Carnegie or any other university in the US. So the children of India are in a mood to quit India. If you observe any young set of people between the age of 20 and 25, you would find them in a mood of utter desperation. They do not know what to do.

And who is responsible for this? Surely, the generation, which broadly ended its tenure sometime between 1947 and 1955-1960, got us freedom for a song. Gandhiji taught us how to attain freedom against the extremely strongly armed enemy of imperialism without largely using any bullets against them. I sometimes think that Gandhiji almost got us freedom at too cheap a price. This is not out of lack of veneration of Gandhiji's memory. But I do not think we quite appreciate that what we have got is with but little sacrifice from ourselves.

What is the status of election and what does election in India mean? Most of you will not comprehend what an extraordinarily complicated exercise the elections in India constitute. Today the estimated population of India is 900 million people and the number of people on the electoral rolls is of the order of 550 million, 55 crores of people. When we run an election in the whole of the country, it is run to the tune of something like eight lakhs of polling booths situated in cities and towns, situated in villages, situated in forests, situated in Ladakh, situated in Saurashtra and Kutch, situated in Sundarbans, situated in the island territories of India. Access to some of these areas is possible only by helicopters (with the help of Indian Air Force) and at other places like Rajasthan only by camel-back. We employ something like three to four million civilian employees, to run the election. That does not include a single policeman. We need about five to six people in each polling booth, to act as polling officers, one polling officer, two presiding officers, one general-purpose assistant and if Assembly election is also thrown in the bargain we need extra personnel too. So when you run an election we need four million people.

And the total number of staff in the Election Commission as of day before yesterday evening count is 196 people including the Chief Election Commissioner and down to the last cleaner of the office, including two deputies of the status of Joint Secretary to the Government of India, six Secretaries of the status of Deputy Secretary to the Government of India, nine Under Secretaries, twenty-four Section Officers.

People generally ask me this question, "why can't we have a single-day election?" I want to tell you at the outset that as far as I am concerned, as far as the Election Commission is concerned, we are willing to run a one-day election at any time you ask us to do so. Each polling booth, of the eight lakhs of them I mentioned, needs 70 items to be sent to them, ranging from ballot boxes to ballot papers to metal seal wire. I do not think we ever had elections seriously damaged because of either men or material not arriving. Make no mistake about it: the Indian election system, after the Taj Mahal, is one of the seven wonders of the world. That it functions at all is a matter of extraordinary surprise. So when I start breast-beating don't you get away with the impression that I am doing only breast-beating. Hold your heads high and say this is my own, my native land, this is the only country where the electorate may be illiterate but they are not unwise people. They will collect whatever they can, collect from wherever they can — does it sound like somebody else's election speech? I apologise. Bombay is not the safest place to make that kind of speech. They take whatever they can, and do exactly what they want to do and they have now even learnt to cheat the exit poll people. As was proved recently, the exit polls predicted something, and the results were something else. Apparently the Indian voter has become wiser. He knows in his heart of hearts that the vote is his. And he votes exactly as he likes.

Article 324 and subsequent Articles of the Constitution of India confer upon the Election Commission the responsibility for running a free and fair election. It is as simple as that, subject to any laws which Parliament may make on the questions of how to run the elections. For instance, if they say everybody must face the east, as he puts the vote in the ballot box, we will jolly well insist that people get to face the east. If they tell us to face the west, we will make them face the west. That is within the prerogative of Parliament to tell us, "please run the election this way under the Representation of the People Act, 1950 and under the Representation of the People Act, 1951, under the Chief Election Commissioner and other Election Commissioners' Remunerations and Conditions of Service Act and the procedure of the Act as passed in 1991, as recently modified by the ordinance, to tell us how to run the internal business of the Commission." Not to speak of having two more Election Commissioners of the same status and rank as the Chief Election Commissioner. If you kindly send for Article 324 and its subsequent sections Parliament is competent to legislate on how to run the election. Parliament is competent to fix the remunerations, terms and conditions of service of the Chief Election Commissioner and other Election Commissioners. I have not yet seen something in the Constitution which says Parliament is competent to legislate on how the Commission will sweep its floor and fill its water jug. That matter is before Parliament in one sense that the Lok Sabha has passed the enabling, substituting law to replace the ordinance by law, and it is now going to the Rajya Sabha. I hope it will get passed by it.

If it does not before the Rajya Sabha rises on Friday evening, then under the constitutional provisions, the law will become defunct on 17 January. So they have to get it passed and signed by the President before the 17 January. And I hope they succeed. As I have taken it to court, somebody will say, "what is your reaction to a multimember commission?" For God's sake, this is not a new invention. The original Constitution says that the Election Commission shall consist of the Chief Election Commissioner, and such other Election Commissioners as the President may from time to time appoint including regional commissioners. For God's sake, multimember law was passed in 1950 whenever the Constitution was passed. What is new now is that, you have passed the law which says that the Election Commissioner will have the same salary as the Chief Election Commissioner. When you say the Election Commission shall as far as possible allocate work and determine the procedure, it shall always be done by consensus, and if they do not do it by consensus, they will do it by majority. Thank God, they did not say they will do it by *kushti* in the Election Commission lawns. If that is what the pending law is, it is hopefully to be passed by the Rajya Sabha and hopefully the Supreme Court will decide on it.

"What is your reaction?" I am reactionless. Why should I react? It was not deliberate when I went to Pune on the 3rd or 4th of October, and said a 101 Election Commissioners are not going to make any difference to the election procedure. Perhaps, it will help it to take faster decisions if there are 101 people in the Election Commission. I hope you understand what I mean by 'fast'.

Why do you want to reform the election system when it is functioning so well? Whenever there is an election, governments are formed and Governors are active. For once, the Governor's chief occupation is not just to buy a Red Cross flag. The Governor becomes active when an election gets over. He is then to decide whom to call to form the government. Sometimes under President's rule, when the Governors are overzealous and overactive, they appoint DGs of police while the elections are still going on. Would I save much of time by saying that it is much easier to answer the question what is wrong with our elections by replacing it with the question what is right with our elections. Some outstanding political gentlemen from Madras said the Chief Election Commissioner ought to be ashamed of saying that the election process has been reduced to a farce in many senses. At this statement you may rebuke me and say: "Just now you have been beating your breast and patting yourself on the back saying the Indian elections are the world's seventh wonder. But then you say it is a farce."

I will very rapidly talk about the *Dasamahapathaka* of Indian elections — the ten great sins of Indian elections. If anybody does not get the exact count of ten do not blame me because I am not good at numbers.

The rolls are bad. The polling booths are bad. If two people go in, three people have to come out. That's the kind of polling booths we have. Then there is a Model Code of Conduct which in Sanskritized Hindi is called *Acharya Samhita*. The outstanding way in which the Model Code is followed in this country is that every single word of the 'Model Code' is offended. This applies to every party which counts. Now, the amount of places at which the elections are corrupted by misdemeanour is so much that you can write a whole book.

And the Election Commission was like Jesus just till the other day till someone like me came into the scene. "To them that slap thee on thy right cheek, show thine left also," was the Election Commission's motto unwritten. And thereafter whatever decision is given, in any case, does not matter. You will ask me, "why are the parties being allowed to work out propaganda using all kinds of wrong methodologies?" Look at the basic conditions of religion, caste, community, language, subcaste — this is your grandmother's river, that is my grandfather's river. You are a Jat, I am a Yadav. You are a Thakur, I am a Brahmin. You are a Gaud Saraswat, I am Chitpavan Brahmin. Sorry I have to say all this but what can you do to me? Oh, yes, you will impeach me and my answer to those who want to impeach me in good chaste Hindi idiom is *Aa bail mujhe mar*. You want to send me home today, but I did not want your job yesterday.

I can spend the whole morning telling you how rigging becomes booth-capturing. There is a very narrow line which divides the two. When you do not turn away all the polling staff, then it becomes only rigging. But when you wield the stick and chase them out it is booth-capturing. Then in each constituency dozens and dozens of candidates are set up. Therefore when I went to the New Delhi constituency to exercise my franchise for the second time in my life, the ballot paper looked like a sheet from today's newspaper. And I had great difficulty to find out where Rajesh Khanna was and where Shatrughan Sinha was. You had a constituency deep down in the South where there were only 370 candidates, so the ballot paper did not look like a sheet of today's newspaper; it looked like today's edition of the newspaper.

The next problem is how to prevent frivolous candidates. Is it my job to prevent frivolous candidates? Do you want to have democracy in India somewhat like a guided democracy which was prevalent in Nepal till recently? The fundamental principle of democracy is the right to disagree. But then who will say that X is a frivolous candidate and Y is not a frivolous candidate? Are we going to curb the freedom to express dissent in this country? If you permit the control of dissent in the name of frivolous candidates, you will end up by controlling all genuine disagreement. Who has to decide it? The Election Commission should decide it? What rubbish! The Election Commission is endowed with an enormous amount of ignorance. How can we decide who is a genuine candidate?

Who else will decide? The Executive Government will decide? God save the motherland. On the other hand, the political parties set up 20, 30 dummy candidates. Because until the last minute, the Parliamentary forum of that party is not able to decide who is its candidate and that is decided at the last moment of withdrawal. Then one gentleman produces the authorization certificate from the State Authorised Representative, and another gentleman produces from the National Authorised Representative and I am asked to decide who is the genuine party candidate in the election.

Then I am dragged to the court saying that you did not decide the genuine candidate from the non-genuine candidate. Mr. H.K.L. Bhagat was nominated by the All-India Congress Committee to authorise candidates for the Delhi elections. He authorised 'X'. One or two hours later, Mr. 'Y' brought a letter from the General Secretary of the All-India Congress Committee, Mr. Nawal Kishore Sharma, who said, "I withdraw the delegation to Mr. H.K.L. Bhagat only in respect of this constituency and I hereby nominate Mr. 'Y'". And my poor returning officer was tearing his hair to find out 'X' or 'Y'. He decided 'X' was 'X' and that 'X' was good enough. So in our election there are frivolous candidates, too many candidates, and there are ballot papers which look like newspapers. It certainly results in an enormous cost because we print ballot papers on security paper. If you have 365 candidates you not only waste paper but as in the case of Tamil Nadu election we ran out of symbols. The symbols used were pen and ink bottle, black-board, radio, television, motor-cycle, ordinary cycle, all sorts of things. But at the end of it, they ran out of symbols. We said, "you can devise, whatever symbol so long as you don't use animals for symbols." Once we tried the experiment of animals also in Tamil Nadu. Party 'A' had the pigeon, and party 'B' had the chicken as symbols. Each party used to bring animals of the other party and wring its neck on top of the dais. Since I was the Secretary of Environment, I told the election people, please, for God's sake, save the birds and animals. We still have a party with a lion as a symbol. But thank God it can't be brought on the stage for its head to be wrung off.

The Chief Minister of one State made a statement: "It matters very little who actually wins in the election. Once the counting has been done, the returning officer will stand up and announce the name of only our own candidate. Even if he reads out a different name by mistake he will never get as near as the Patna railway station. Supposing he does manage to get there, somehow, his chances of reaching Delhi would be nil." Free elections anybody?

Fundamental to the entire question of running a fair and free election is the neutrality of the civil servant. The civil servant at the state level, at district level, at multidistrict level, at subsubdistrict level, at *thana* level, at constable level, is supposed to be ruthlessly impartial in this game. I want to tell you that more than anything else this country's elections have been most heavily damaged by a partisan civil service. They have become contaminated, collusive and corrupt. Some of them are looking for petty pelf for office. "You know, I would like to go to Economic Affairs Ministry, or Commerce Ministry because that way I can go to Switzerland to negotiate GATT."

For GATT sake! "Weren't you a civil servant yourself till yesterday? How does it lie in your mouth to speak about this?"

My civil service career is a closed book. You can open it if you can. I shall not help you. You can't compel me to give evidence against myself. Let me tell you about my first encounter with a Minister. In 1957 I was in my first job with an independent charge. One day, in the middle of May, when I was all suited and booted, coated and buttoned up to my neck, the then Minister of Police, Revenue and PWD decided to take me in his borrowed car. Probably that was my first and last chance to get into a brand new Dodge. Those days the Madras Ministers used to borrow cars from one of the biggest transport organisations. On our way he suddenly turned on me and said, "why are you working against the Congress?" I said, "Sir, I was not aware of working against anybody."

"Then in that case will you withdraw the police prosecution against the head of so-and-so village? Because he is the husband of the Tehsil Congress Committee President."

I said, "Sir, you give me a written order, and on that basis I will withdraw the charge." Then the Minister kept silent for five minutes and asked the driver to stop and drop me in the middle of nowhere. I stood under a tree for 105 minutes before my jeep turned up because it was an old war service jeep and the maximum speed it could pick up was ten miles an hour. But I persistently and tenaciously followed the Minister for the rest of the day. This is not yesterday's phenomenon or today's phenomenon.

The elections are damaged in every possible way. Over the years, the civil service, partly by fear, partly by inducement, partly by something else, has been reduced to tools in the hands of party politicians in every State. I have six national parties, 43 State-recognised parties and 300 unrecognised parties. Whoever is in government, it makes no difference whether it is party 'A', party 'B', party 'C', party 'D', party 'E', party 'F'. The misuse of the civil service for purpose of electioneering work has reached appalling proportions in this country. When in November, a Union Minister was making a speech, the District Magistrate sent him a chit saying, "Sir, it is 5 o'clock, you are past the time of electioneering. Will you please come down?" And the Minister read the chit to the entire audience, which was not very large, of course, and said: "Who is this DM to tell me when to stop my speech." So the DM sent the second chit saying "in approximately two minutes from now two constables will guide you down the steps." Whereupon the Minister came down fuming and sat on the ground and said, "I am going on a fast unto death", and the DM said, "I will give you every facility."

Let us have more laws for this country, particularly on electoral reforms. We would be much better off with a law which enables the Commission to audit [accounts] and point the finger of corruption on people who spend money in excess. In Delhi elections the other day, there was a lady who fought the poll. May the lady remain nameless. The total electorate was 50,000 and this lady candidate told me personally, in my drawing room, that she spent only Rs. 55 lakhs. What a mere difference — 50,000 and 55 lakhs.

Government had fixed the limit at about Rs. 1.5 lakhs as the ceiling for a Parliament seat. You cannot run an election on that amount. The Thane constituency near Bombay has a total electorate of 1.8 million voters. If you want to send a post-card to each person it will cost more than Rs. 1.5 lakhs. Not that the post-card will reach, depending on whether the postmen are on strike or not. But that is a different story.

You have fixed an undesirable, unlikely, impractical limit. You then proceed to ignore it. There is a facility which is now going to go on: that every candidate is to file a return of his expenses, within 30 days of the declaration of the results. And he will sign a statement which says: "I spent Rs.250 on the deposit and Rs. 233 on all other expenses, the sum total expenses is Rs. 483."

"But I had noticed multicoloured posters in your constituency. How did they appear?" "Sir, it was sent to me by my friends." "But you have 25 jeeps with your symbol running all over the constituency. Where did they come from?"

"The jeep-*wallahs* had sent them to me."

The election expenses account *tamasha* is the most elaborate joke and it is one single, largest source of corruption in the country. Rajaji warned about this way back in the fifties when he was jobless. He said, "for God's sake Panditji, you are expanding the permit licence raj." And it required the IMF and Manmohan Singh to come and undo it for us. Now that is history. Or geography, maybe. Why does a businessman have cupidity? He has cupidity because the fundamental objective of business is to succeed. Whether there is morality in it or not is a secondary issue. Ultimately, the balance sheet is written. If the ink is black, they will do a *shabaash* for the Managing Director. If the ink is red, they will throw him out mercilessly.

I am not here to talk about the morality of business. I am sure one of these days you will have a seminar on the subject. But that will have to wait until Manmohan Singh is finished with his work. How do you control this? A simple amendment in the law which enables us to investigate into the details of the accounts will do. I will narrate to you an autobiographical story. The first impeachment notion (not motion) against me came in July of 1991, immediately after the elections were over. Somebody in the Government said, "keep a low profile for sometime and go to America." They did not give me a rupee. I spent my hard-earned money and went to America. I hid myself in the houses of nieces and nephews for a month. And when I came back, they said, "Oh, you've come back but we still want you to keep a low profile." I said, considering the totality of my size, it is very difficult for me to be of low profile. It was resumed after the elections of October-November of 1991. They said we are going to impeach you. They also said, "we want to protect you and the job." To that I said, "you look after the job." The leaders of the Opposition came and said, "on behalf of the government" ambassadorships and governorships are still available. In this connection I will repeat the joke which I repeat everywhere. I said, "the only way I will ever become the governor is for my wife to become a governess and we have not found a suitable child. And the nearest I have ever been to an ambassador is my staff car. I will accept nothing."

"What can I then give you?"

I said, "Sir, the answer is in the question. Anything you can give is *ipso facto* unacceptable." Then I told him a proverb in Tamil which says you go and sit under a palm tree and drink the best Haryana milk, the passersby will still think you are drinking toddy. Somebody came and politely said, "we will make you the General Secretary of the party because in six months' time XYZ is going to become the

President and XYZ worships the ground on which you walk."
What price freedom?

Today, you need a better Chief Election Commissioner.
Of that I have no doubt. You need what a gentleman said
yesterday, a less idiosyncratic Chief Election Commissioner.
Because you do not know which direction this unguided
missile will fly next. But if you want to reform the electoral
system, you have to improve the rolls. Even if you are willing
to improve the rolls, the polling booths are badly located. In
the same building there are ten polling booths and I do not
know whether to go to classroom 'A' or classroom 'B' or
classroom 'C'. The civil servants are not neutral. There is
rigging, there is booth-capturing, there are political parties,
with their misbehaviour, there are hundreds of candidates,
many of whom are frivolous. Why do parties set up frivolous
candidates? Because then behind each frivolous candidate you
get passes for two cars from the returning officer. If you have
50 frivolous candidates, you get 100 more cars to go round
the constituency without let or hindrance. Then you can put
50 of your people inside the polling booths as polling agents.
Then you can put another 50 of them in the counting booth.
And as I told you in many cases the party is not able to
decide, which is the candidate at the last minute and even
beyond, and leaves it to the tender mercies of the returning
officer to decide who is party 'A's official candidate and who
is not.

I am not in the least trying to hide the many many defects.
I told you the lack of impartiality on the part of the civil
servants is very damaging. But I can assure you that without
passing many more laws, if not any more law, we can control
most of this if only you have men with backbone at
appropriate places. Why did Parliament say that the Chief
Election Commissioner can be got rid of only by
impeachment? Our founding fathers were not jokers. They
knew that at some time if the necessity arises, this man will
need to display that he is vertebrate. If three honest judges

sit together and say, "Mr. Seshan, why did you postpone Punjab elections at the last moment?" I tell you the answer, which is the lone answer because the matter is still pending before the Speaker on an impeachment motion. The day the Speaker decided either to hand it over to the three judges, after a vote of Parliament, or he says the file is closed, I will tell the country why I postponed the Punjab elections, scheduled for the 22 June.

Once in an article I was compared to a station master as if I was waving a red flag for postponements of elections. Do you think I take pleasure in cancellations and postponements? One Chief Minister says, "I will give schemes worth Rs. 500 crores." Another Chief Minister says, "I will give schemes worth Rs. 25 crores." The third Chief Minister writes to me and says, "the Hindus and Muslims are about to kill each other in thousands in Ottapalam." The Central Government confirms this to me and warns me that the law and order situation in Ottapalam is so grave, the communal situation is so grave that I should postpone the election. Two days later when the right honourable Chief Minister is asked in the Assembly: "Did you ask for a postponement?" the right honourable Chief Minister says, "we have made no such request." I can publish the documentation but how many Chief Ministers are equal to one Chief Election Commissioner? Or rather how many Chief Ministers can one Chief Election Commissioner equal?

In Assam because I got rid of the foreigners, Mr. Saikia is angry. Mr. Jyoti Basu is generally angry. Mr. Laloo Yadav is always angry. Smt. Jayalalitha is very angry. Vijay Bhaskar Reddy implored me to ensure that his election was conducted before 8 April, on which day he would have ceased to become the Chief Minister. And till the elections were on he kept quiet and the moment the elections got over, he said, "I shall expose Seshan." I am reminded of a little sticker pasted on the rear of an American truck when streaking was at its best. It said "streakers of the world beware, your end is in sight." So I have friends all over.

The electoral law does need reform and it is a fundamental law of physics that those in power will never give up power, whether they are elected or whether they are appointed. This is the fourth law of thermodynamics.

India is destined for greatness. About 300 years ago it was one of the most advanced countries in the world. Today you find that you cannot pay your electricity bill without paying 10 per cent extra. You cannot get gas replacement, you cannot get a telephone connection. You cannot get all kinds of things without additional cash. I said we were one of the most developed countries, if not the developed country, in the world 300 years ago. But history is good for lunch, it is not good for sleep.

India's diversity is fantastically amazing. We have several hundred languages. Some with script, some without script. We have several religions. Every religion of the world is available in this country. In each religion there are so many subreligions that the same Hindu will find satisfaction by cutting a goat (because he cannot cut a child) in order to propitiate it to Kali. There are other Hindus (I am not talking of Jains) who would put a mask on their face so that unwary insects would not go into their mouth. All of this is my Hinduism. Hinduism is not this temple or that temple. Hinduism is a way of life. The fundamental ethos of Bharat was tolerance. Today we have nothing but intolerance — caste intolerance, linguistic intolerance, subcaste intolerance, religious intolerance. I am saying this to tell you that if somebody comes and asks, "why don't we go away from democracy"?, he is asking a non-question. According to engineering principles if you tie up a body by rigid joints, the body will twist, if not break. The Indian body politic is full of so many joints — religious joints, caste joints, linguistic joints. But what you need is a loosely joined thing and that is available only in a democracy.

True democracy will function only on the basis of two pillars. One pillar is the pillar of the rule of law which has all but disappeared. Today it is so difficult to file an FIR or to fight a case. I have not come here to commit contempt of the Judiciary; the Judiciary is my last sanctuary. True democracy can, therefore, subsist on the rule of law and the expression of free will of the people. The elections are the only method, just as the rule of law which is incorruptible, which is fast, which is quick, this is the only way in which the rule of law can be established. The only way in which you can establish democracy by the will of the people is by the conduct of a free and fair election. QED Mr. T.N.Seshan. No. QED Election Commission. The present elections are corrupted by money, by caste, by religion, by criminalisation, by corruption and the bamboo frame. People in power, whether elected or appointed, will not leave, except by *ek aur dhakka*. Does that sound familiar? One can make philosophical claims to an audience. I have prepared this for young people but even for old people this is true.

Let us abjure violence as a method, not because I am a Gandhian. But you don't have to be a Gandhian to say that if you will settle disputes by the strength of the fist, if you rule by the sword, you will perish by the sword. And even if you are rich, please don't go and buy Rigley chewing gum at the airport for Rs. 100 a packet. I have seen children of rich people travelling by first class airbus or J-class airbus to come to Bombay to see *Khalnayak* on the day of the release in whatever that cinema is near Worli. So, for God's sake, even if you are rich, do not show it off. Let us set an example for ourselves on small things — on dowry, on linguistic fanaticism, on religious fanaticism. Some people say let us get rid of the following kinds of people from the surface of this country. How will you get rid of them? They are in *every mohalla*, every street. Down first floor is so-and-so, second floor is so-and-so, third floor is so-and-so. How will you get rid of them? Even practical politics makes it impossible. I am not saying somebody should be pampered. Nobody should be pampered.

Almost finally, I have a request to make. Let us all take a resolve through the Citizens' Consensus for Democracy or National Consensus that we will not vote on any criteria except merit hereafter. Is the man straight? Does the man have integrity? I don't have the power to change the law by which criminals cannot contest the election and I can scream until I'm blue in the face, but it is unlikely that Parliament will pass such a law. One of the gravest disasters in Indian polity is the full-time professional politician who has no other way of living. What was Panditji? Panditji got a tripos in Cambridge, he was a Bar-at-Law and he was called to the Inner Temple. What was Gandhiji? He was a Bar-at-Law. What was Sardar Patel, what was Motilal Nehru, what was Azad, what was Jinnah who started writing our history but ended up rewriting our geography? They were all men who sacrificed what they could have done otherwise in order to come and serve the country. Today, the gentlemen and ladies who represent us on the floors of the legislatures are people who are full-time, 25-hour politicians.

There is simply no point in saying, who should get to the Assembly. Have you heard the story about the twins in Lucknow? A pair of twins was about to come out of the womb of a mother. Each child told the other child, "*pehle aap*" because Lucknow is notorious for its politeness. Ultimately, the mother died. A majority of us keep saying, "no no, a lawyer should get into the Assembly", "judges should get into the Assembly", "retired civil servants should get into the Assembly." Who are you to tell others what to do? Do it yourself. Set yourself up as a candidate. At the most you may lose your deposit of Rs. 250 saved from all your pension and savings. To make the totality of expenditure completely transparent, the days should go whereby a lady who has filed a return that she has spent Rs. 483 comes and tells me that she has spent Rs. 55 lakhs. And here we sit gumless and toothless. When I said I am going to audit the expenditure, people asked me, "after you audit and if you find any irregularity, what will you do?" I will go to the tree and do *tapasya*? No, you just wait and watch. I don't reveal trumps until it is time to rough a deal. To rough a hand, I will not tell you what trumps are. Is that good bridge language? I don't play any bridge, because I don't know how to wink eyes at the partner.

Somebody told me: "Parties submit manifestos but they never carry them out." Has any of you asked the same gentleman when he comes back for electionereing, "what happened to your last time's manifesto? The things you said you will do, how come none of it has happened? What has your party done?" Should you have the right to recall? That is a two-edged sword. It can be used to get rid of honest people. The dishonest people will still stay because of the fundamental laws of centrifuging. The heavier particles will settle down. If you shake a centrifuge, lighter particles will fly off. Slag will settle at the bottom. You will have a Parliament of slags. Ultimately you will need only Oliver Cromwell who went into Parliament in 1726 and said, "in the name of God, go." Please let us not lead to that condition because you are on the edge of that precipice ....

We have national grids of all kinds.

We have a national grid of intolerance, of language by which, for example, in the Bombay buses (BEST) not only will they put the destinations in Marathi, which I don't mind, but even the bus numbers are put in Marathi numerals. So, I went to a friend and asked, "how shall I reach such-and-such place?" He asked me to take 324 from Chembur. So I went there but as I don't know how to read Devnagri or Marathi numerals, I stood there helplessly till six buses passed. I went back to the friend and said, "no 324 came". He said, "you are illiterate."

We have come to this national level of consensus where language has become a bone of unnecessary fighting, though anybody in his elementary senses would tell you that the fundamental purpose of language is to communicate. If I talk Chinese and you talk Russian, and we are unable to communicate with each other, it ends up in blows in two-and-a-half minutes. The fundamental purpose of language is communication and we have forgotten that in our pursuit of linguistic intolerance; ultimately what is missing in us is the absence of character. And as an author wrote: "When even one piece of soil of Europe goes into the water, it is as if some part of me went away." And he ended up the passage by the famous saying: "Ask not for whom the bell tolls, it tolls for thee."

We have sat as a collective nation of 900 million people, watching *hame kya lena dena hai*. I can give you a thousand examples of corruption and you will react by giving me 10,000 examples of corruption and the next gentleman will give me 100,000 examples of corruption. But which one of us has lifted a little finger to say that this is not done. How can I ask a question and not wait for an answer? Has the Press in India done so? Has the Press in India highlighted corruption? I don't know. Who am I to ask the question, much less to wait for an answer? Today you can point a finger and say, "politicians are all right, civil servants are not all right." Are professionals alright? What about doctors, lawyers, accountants? "So have you come here like a Cassandra to preach doom?" No way. I have not come to prophesise doom. My fundamental premise is that India is born to greatness. You may rewrite decent pieces of geography and decide whether Chakma is a refugee or whether some language is a language or whether some script is a script. But India is bound to a destiny of greatness.

We are very good at writing algorithms. Indian software is fantastic. Indian hardware is even better. And we know bio-technology as well as next man in the world. But all this will serve you only if there is a canvas and today that canvas is in danger. And one of the fundamental places at which you need to put stitches is in elections. And the most important places in which you want to put a stitch are expenses — corrupt expenses; the country has a right to demand an impartial civil service to administer this. And when you see something wrong, for God's sake don't keep quiet. The 900 million people are required to act as the eyes and ears of the election process if you are going to prevent this *Dhandhli* from continuing. I have done ramblings and wanderings even if they have not led to a coherent completion. It is that those in power will not do anything which will be tantamount to reduction of power. Those with money will not pass laws which reduce money power. You will have to compel it. Civil servants are by nature what they are. You have the right to expect and tell the Election Commission: "Give us a poll which is complete. Give us polling stations which are reasonable. Give us quick counting, give the Press adequate access." The complaint of the Press is that I prevented them from having adequate access. That will remain for another day to tell the story. Make your entire election process as transparent as is humanly possible but not so transparent as to become naked of course.

7

University of the World

What does one say to a set of children who are about to step out. Not yet quite, but they are about to reach the outer doors of the wide, wide world. You have finished the 12th standard of study, and I have no doubt at all that every one of you will come out with outstanding colours, which will do justice to yourself, to your parents, to your teachers and to the school which has nurtured you during these long years. I have no doubt at all that every child who had his or her citation read, who has made his or her promises, who has lit the lamp which binds this country together, every child who has taken blessings from the elders, will go out and be a shining lamp to the rest of the country and to the rest of the world.

Speech made at the farewell function of Blue Bells School, New Delhi.

As they stand at the threshold of a future, I want to congratulate them. I want to wish them well. I want to tell them how exhilarating life is. Don't be weighed down by the feeling that this world is a cruel world, it is a bad world, it is a difficult world. But ahead of all these, this is an exhilarating world. This is a world of abounding opportunities, whether you have studied science, commerce or arts, whether you have done sports, theatre, written stories or poems. All these are going to stand you in outstanding stead as you go up further into the portals of the absolutely largest university, namely, the university of the world.

I know that the young people of today are confused. Sometimes they look back on the school and think the world is roses, roses all the way. These children whom I suspect, if my arithmetic is not very wrong, are of 16-17 years of age, must be confused by the thought as to what kind of world are they stepping into. So long as they were under the parental umbrella of the school, all that mattered was to move from class 1 to 2, to 3, to 4, and so on to 11 and on to 12 under the extraordinary parental guidance of madam principal, whoever she may be. I am delighted to see that of the entire faculty, only a hopeless minority is men, the rest of them are all women and that undoubtedly must account for the fact that the school is an outstanding one. Whether because it is an outstanding school that the majority of the teachers are ladies or because all the teachers are ladies, the school is outstanding, there is no question that in their combination, we have brought forth the best of 75 or 80 children.

What will you think of today? Will you think of Blue Bells? Will you think of madam founder Princy? What will you call these good teachers who have come across to see, to join our hopes and sorrows and share them? What kind of families are you from? Are these families going to exert on you enormous pressure to think that you must necessarily become an engineer or a doctor, whereas what you would like to do is maybe theatre, maybe video, or maybe something else.

I want to appeal to the parents, as a parent who has no child, please for God's sake don't pressurise these children. Let these children blossom into flowers. We didn't have 12th standard we had 11 standards or 13 standards, whichever way you look at it. I suppose your 12th is roughly equivalent to what we had in 13th. The outstanding educationists of this country did an enormous piece of algebra and decided that $11 + 2 + 2$ having been changed into $10 + 2 + 3$ is an enormous change. So, I am talking of $11 + 2$ because we were slow people. Therefore, it took us 13 years what it takes you 12 years to do and when I finished that stage in 1947, 47 years ago, there were not one-hundredth of the opportunities which are before you today. The opportunities to study in an enormous variety of substances and things, not only of physics and chemistry, not only of mathematics and statistics, not only of philosophy and psychology, not only of politics and political science and public administration — but a whole new variety of subjects, not to speak of computers and biotechnology. Today, a million doors are about to open themselves to you. And don't you ever believe if somebody tells you, even at the height of his or her parental pressure, that the world is a difficult world where you would not fit in. You will jolly well fit in. One fact was necessary: it was the fact that you are outstanding kids. You had an outstanding school, you had an outstanding atmosphere and if what I have imbibed of the school during the last one hour is any indication, I am sorely jealous of the kind of atomosphere in which you have been brought up. No, it is not a jealousy born of anything else, but a jealousy born of saying good Lord, why didn't I have a school 47 years ago which looked similar to this?

Your school has done you proud; your school has given each of you a citation and in two or three months from today, you will go out into the world to choose your own professions and your own calling. What calling shall I choose for myself? Shall I do theatre, shall I do philosophy, shall I do physics, shall I do chemistry, shall I do engineering, shall I do medicine? What shall I do? I must tell you that considering the extraordinary amount of confusion and complexity which is engendered by your present stage of education, there is a truth about this country and about your future which is that it is absolutely outstanding. Don't let anybody allow you to wear you down into the belief that your future is anything but the brightest of the brightest lamps that you have lit today. Yes, there is an amount of dross out there, there is an amount of corruption out there, there is an amount of inhumanity out there, there is a lack of compassion out there, there are all kinds of wrong things out there. So, you are fighting many other confusions. You are at that age where physically you are in confusion. You are at that stage where your education is going to open a thousand outlets into which you don't know which outlet you would go to, where you would get caught, where you would prosper. I am told the school does a fairly good amount of career guidance and counselling. I am sure it is an enormous advantage that you have.

So, what does a Chief Election Commissioner do to come and advise children, 80 children who are going to step out into the world? I can only tell you one thing, picked up from several places, picked up from several books: "Believe in what you do. Do what you believe in." The world is good enough, the world is large enough, the world is rich enough, the world is sagacious enough to give you scope for doing all that you want to do so long as you do what you believe in, and you believe in what you do. I cannot think of any greater advice for you today except to suggest that whatever avocation you choose, may you become the most skilful in that avocation. May you become the most outstanding in that avocation. Let it not be said that this child came from this school but was the second best in his or in her chosen discipline of learning and working. May the good Lord show you the paths.

But a skill in action, a skill in discipline, a skill in profession, is not that which is enough to make you a round and whole human being. That which is necessary is to understand and appreciate the fundamental values of life. That value in life which teaches you the difference between the right and the wrong. It doesn't matter what religion you believe in, every single religion — be it Hinduism, be it Christianity, be it Islam, be it Sikhism, be it Jainism — every single religion in this country, in the world, teaches there is a right way and there is a wrong way. May the Lord grant it to you that in all that you do, you will choose the right way in preference to the wrong way, even when the choice, the adherence to the right way, results in what looks like temporary disadvantage and temporary suffering. Mankind will survive only on the basis of the unassailable belief that ultimately the right will win, ultimately the truth will win.

The world today is divided into all kinds of fragments — fragments of religion, caste, language, geography, states and countries and towns and villages. An what have you learnt in the last 12 years? You have learnt *Vasudhaiva Kutumbakam*. That statement says my family is the whole of the 'vasudha'. What is my family? My family is the entire universe. *Vasudha* is not merely the planet. It goes even beyond the planet to say that all that pervades God's creation is my family. Have compassion towards the weak. Compassion, not merely of the physically weak, those who are mentally weak, those who are financially weak, those who are weak economically, those who are weak because of social oppression, not only of human beings, but of all that this planet pervades. May God grant you the light today to believe that compassion, that right, that honesty, that truth, these are the ultimate values, not merely the science which you have learnt or the commerce you have learnt or the arts which you have learnt, or the sports you have learnt, or the theatre which you have learnt. They are necessary in their own ways. And may each one of you become what the Bhagwad Gita says

यद्यदाचरतिश्रेष्ठो	*Yadyadācharati Sreshtō*
तत्तदेपेतरोजनः	*Tattadevētarō Janaah*
सय प्रमाणंकुरुते	*Sa Yat Pramānam Kurutē*
लोकस्तदनुवर्तते ।।	*Lokastadanu Vartate*

Do whatever the 'Shreshtha' does; 'Shreshtha' is not merely the person who has got the best marks in the CBSE exam. Yes it is one qualification necessary to be called 'the Shrestha'. A 'Shreshtha' is not merely the gentleman who jumps highest in the high jump. The 'Shreshtha' is not merely the girl who is best in elocution or best in music, best in dancing, best in something else. The 'Shreshtha' is somebody whose fundamental values are screwed on the right way so that the world "*Yadyatācharati Sreshtō*"— follows whatever the path the *Shrestha* follows. "*Tattadevētarō Janaah*" — that is what the other people follow. "*Sat Yat Pramānam Kurutē*" — what he decides is the right thing to do. "*Lokastadanu Vartate*" — the whole world will follow him or her.

May all that you have learnt in the last 12 years stand you in good stead, not only for the next 3 or 5 or 7 or 9 years, you may go into MBBS, and then go into MD, you may do engineering and then go into research. You may do biotechnology and go on to a doctorate. You may merely go into photography and become a cameraman or a camera-woman, or a 'camera person' as somebody taught me to say. So, whatever you do in whichever walk of life, you may merely become a good father or a good mother. In whatever you put your hands to, may the world be able to say that "this was the complete human being." *Into that heaven of freedom, let this country awake.*

8

"The Rich Get Richer, The Poor Get Children"

came to know Dr. Chandran Devanesan, approximately 45 years ago in 1949, when I entered the portals of the Madras Christian College in search of physics. Devanesan was not a man of physics. He was a man of history. Devanesan was a man of kindness. He was a man of gentility. He was a man of erudition. He was a man of scholarship. Above all he was a human being of a biblical nature. I spent six years in the Madras Christian College, three years as a student and three years later as a teacher. And during those six years, I don't remember having seen Prof. Chandran Devanesan ever get angry. If there was a human being who could forgive as a true Christian can, that was Chandran Devanesan. He was

---

Dr. Devanesan Memorial Lecture delivered in Madras on 26 March 1994.

born in 1917 and when he died in 1982, he was 65 years old. Erudition and scholarship sat lightly on him and he could be easily mistaken for a plebeian individual despite all the erudition with which he was bedecked. The last time I remember seeing him was when he was battling in the North-East of India as the Vice-Chancellor of the Hill University. And I still remember that the problems of the North-East, which have distressed much bigger minds and much greater capabilities and knowledge, had not distressed him. He was hopeful. He was wishing that the North-East would get what it deserved to get like the rest of India, or perhaps even more. I have no intention of spending much more time talking about Chandran Devanesan. Because all that had mattered then and all that matters now is that many of us were blessed to have known him.

What does one speak in memory of Chandran Devanesan?

As I have mentioned, what one is reminded of when talking in memory of Devanesan is that he had the Christian virtues of humility, of compassion, of discipline, of integrity, of dedication. I can go on listing those virtues which are desperately the need of humanity today. Where do you begin when speaking of these virtues? Today, the world is in a state of great *andhkara*. Wherever you look the forces of evil seem to be taking over from the other forces which you can think of collectively. The population of the world is somewhere slightly higher than 4.5 billion people. There is every prospect that in the next less than 25 years it will be 9 billion people. Population is growing at the rate of 3 per cent per year. Those of us who know geometrical progression will know that it will then take approximately 24 to 25 years to double the population and, therefore, in the year of grace, maybe by A.D. 2025 the world will have 9 to 10 billion people, and maybe there would be just enough room for standing. But why think of 25 years from now? Let us think of the next few years.

It is of relevance to India because on the 1st of July A.D. 2001 our population is going to be a billion people. And it is certain that on the 1st of July A.D. 2020, India's population as it stands today with its present geographic boundaries will be higher than even that of China. So whenever somebody talks of Chinese statistics I take it with a pinch of salt. Will the virtues for which the human being distinguished himself from the jungle beast still survive when they are not even surviving in 1994? Where are the human virtues today? Where somebody who has access to high-power weapons in the United States will pick up the weapons, walk into a little school, open fire and kill 25 children for no reason at all, except that *ipso facto* they described him as mentally disturbed. Where in the world are we spending billions of dollars on armaments and weaponry while child after child is dying a cruel death of starvation in Africa, in parts of Asia? Even today in parts of Europe, man's inhumanity to man has rendered it impossible for people to get supplies of food for months together. It requires the United Nations mission of determined capability to reach a convoy of food into the battled land of Sarajevo. Where in the world are we not finding the fruits of this human degradation, where man's inhumanity to man has reached proportions which are truly indescribable? Yet they claim that they are Hindus. They are Muslims. Did any religion tell us to go and kill thy neighbour? Is it not true that every religion taught us to love thy neighbour as thyself? What is the solution to this? For every brutality, there is a greater brutality, there is a greater weapon. Human ingenuity, human wisdom, human cruelty have led us to killing thousands of people who have nothing whatsoever to do with each other except friendship and happiness.

Where did the history of India begin? My history did not begin with Lord Robert Clive. My history did not begin with the Governors-General and Viceroys of India. My history did not begin between the 14th and 15th August midnight when Pandit Nehru stood on the floor of Parliament and said in sonorous language: "Long years ago, we made a tryst with destiny...while the world sleeps, India will awake...". India had woken up earlier but it had gone to sleep in between. It was woken up again. Would it be correct to say that Gandhiji won us freedom at almost a throwaway price?

Did we get freedom in this country at a price which has led us to believe that freedom in the language of those who use English badly today is priceless? Freedom has no price for most people in the country today. It required Gandhiji to fast umpteen times, and to go to Dandi to pick up a handful of salt before we could attain political freedom. It required thousands of others to go to jail, to fast, to get beaten up. When you talk about people being beaten up, my memory does not go merely to Panditji or Sardar Patel. It does not go merely to Maulana Abdul Kalam Azad or various other names. It goes in front of the computer console in front of your eyes. It goes to Pandit Gobind Ballabh Pant being brutally beaten in 1928, to live the rest of his life with a shake all over his body. How many of us have been to the Cellular Jail in the Andamans to see what kind of conditions those people lived in? How many of us remember General Dyer killing people within the confines of Jallianwala Bagh? How many of us bring back to mind the image of VOC? How many of us bring back to mind the king in deep down Tirunelveli who agreed that he would much rather be master in chains than yield? How many of us believe that a gentleman in the west of India said: "Freedom is my birth right?" How many of us believe in Bhagat Singh and his companions, who went up to the gallows, without lowering their head for one second? How many of us remember what price we paid in order to get this liberty?

And today, people are talking hardly 47 years later of at least wanting a dictatorship, if not return of foreign control. Who has brought us to this pitiable pass? What significant things did we earn and achieve? What significant things have we lost?

A country which was going about with a begging bowl at the turn of Independence today exports a certain quantity of rice and wheat. We exported cotton until the cry of handloom weavers stopped it. Today milk is flowing in this country and we can export a little of milk products. And yet is it right to say that in this country, the rich get richer, the poor get children. Between 1947 and 1993-94, we have grown from 350 million people to 900 million people. There is no doubt that on 1 July 2000 as I mentioned earlier, we will be a billion people — a hundred crores of people. Do you know that on 1 July A.D. 2001 of the thousand million people this country has, 400 million will be in urban areas — an urban population higher than in the rest of the world put together?

And where will they live? Delhi is bursting at the seams with a population which is now 9.5 million. It will become 12 million before A.D. 2000. Bombay and Calcutta are gone cases. And of this population in Bombay or Delhi or Calcutta, today 45 per cent live in desperate shanty towns. It was not fashionable when Rajaji said that don't try to eliminate the slums, improve them, give the slum-dwellers better housing. Because Rajaji was unwanted and you criticised him. Then you appointed a board and called it a Slum Clearance Board, and very rapidly you changed it.

On the industrial front, how much have we achieved? India is now called the tenth most industrialised country in the world. Industrial progress has been truly phenomenal for our country which made the coarsest of cloth. We now make the most modern cloth. We know all about computers, we know all about biotechnology. We know about biochemistry and bioengineering. We make rockets, we make satellites. Our own satellites give us programme after programme. What do we not know about which the rest of world does not know? And yet we have other kinds of progress to our credit.

Today no couple can afford to think of conceiving a child until they have decided where that child would get school admission, not to speak of college, and medical college or engineering college, or the IIT. In 47 years of educational improvement what did this country do? They said we are going to go vocational but not one college has a single piece of vocational equipment. When Chandran Devanesan was Principal of the Madras Christian College not once did he have to worry about how to pay teachers' salary for the next month. Today Francis Sunder Raj is sitting in the chair for another couple of months. He is desperately praying that in the next two months he will be able to pay salary without difficulty because the University Grants Commission has thrown up its hands. Forty-seven years of educational planning has led us to a situation where education in India today is neither fish nor flesh nor good red herring.

As for elementary education our Constitution says that all children between the ages of 9 and 14 will have universal compulsory education. What kind of education are you providing? In 1947, the pupil-teacher ratio in the most backward villages of this country was one teacher for 40 children. Today it is one teacher for 80 children. How many *acharyas* are left in the country? I am not talking of those *acharyas* who are by birth *acharyas*. I am talking of those *acharyas* who are *acharyas* by profession. How many of them are fit for being treated as gods? Is it true or not that in school after school, and college after college, the teacher just comes into the classroom, opens a textbook at page 101 and says "pages 101 to 151 is today's lesson. Next week there will be a test. Those of you who want to know more about the subject come to my house tomorrow morning at 6.30 for coaching?"

Is it also true or not that question papers leak all over this country and the entire effort of the university authorities is to suppress the truth of the leakage, not the leakage itself? Is it true that teachers in this country value papers by weight and not by wisdom? Was this what we learnt for 3000 years? India's great culture comes from *gurukula*. Today while the

Registrar doesn't know who is the Vice-Chancellor, the Vice-Chancellor can't get into the building, and universities go without Vice-Chancellors. What pretty pass have we brought education in this country to?

Did you know that the universities of India are autonomous? They are autonomous of what? They are autonomous of wisdom. They are autonomous of freedom. Not autonomous of control. In Madras there are students who come out with a literature honours degree but can't write even one page without several mistakes in spelling and grammar. Someone said the other day, "but Sir, we are very good in Tamil". I never studied a word of Tamil for one day in any school. My entire knowledge of Tamil was acquired through filling a cross-word competition in the *Ananda Viketan* at the age of eight. That is all the Tamil I learnt. But would I be correct if I told you that many students can't even write a page of Tamil without mistakes in writing, mistakes in spelling, mistakes in grammar?

How many of our children know the fundamentals of physics, chemistry, mathematics, the fundamentals of any subject at all? But do I hold the children responsible? "Today's children are poorer in intellect than you and I were when we were children." Rubbish! Today's children are infinitely more intelligent because the very act of survival needs on their part a degree of alacrity, and ability and intellect and skill, which we didn't need in those days to pass through whatever we passed through. And yet a large number of children are left here to become clerks and bus conductors with MAs and M Scs. A small number of them go to Florida, go to Texas. So we are a producing centre for America to get cheap labour and the Indian scientist, the Indian writer, the Indian economist goes and works for one-tenth of the wages which the Americans would have to pay for themselves. I know thousands of young Indians in the United States who ignore themselves, and their families to slog in the office. Because the Americans have found out that Indians make excellent indentured labour. As in an earlier generation, they took us to the Fiji Islands, West Indies, and to other parts of the world to act as indentured labour to cut cane. Today India's most outstanding intellectuals are going to the United States to cut "cane".

Do you blame the young people that they are going to cut cane in the Sun Valley of Florida or in the Sunrise Valley of California? How can you blame them? They are sick and tired of what goes on here in the name of democracy, what goes on here in the name of education, what goes on here in the name of technology. I have spent a large part of my service life in the Science Departments — atomic energy, space, oil and environment. My long association with science and technology tells me that the greatest enemy of science in India is the senior scientist. Would I be correct to summarise the educational status in India in a single sentence — that of all corruption in India, nothing is more corrupt than the educational system.

I can go on in the same vein about the state of health in this country. "Oh. We have got rid of plague." No. Plague is coming back. Small-pox is coming back. No one believes we got rid of malaria. We have mosquitoes, immune to all pesticides that you have devised. Today out of every thousand babies born, 180 die within the first 12 months of existence. Out of the remaining 820 children, another 230 die before they are five. What kind of health care are you talking about? National crash eradication programme, national crash malaria eradication, filaria eradication, tuberculosis eradication, cancer eradication, leprosy eradication. You might as well say national crash 'dash' programme, and replace the 'dash' by any disease you like.

All doctors take an oath when they get somewhere into the medical profession, which is called the Hippocratic oath but many of them spell it differently. It has become a *hypocritic* oath. I go to the doctor and say, "I have a stomach ache." He says, "go and take an electrical encephalogram."

Do you know why he does so? He does so because 40 per cent of the amount charged by the MRI is then kickbacked to the doctor.

Government hospitals are in a desperate condition. Where there are 1000 patients there are 100 deaths. Where there ought to be a 100 nurses, there are just 18. There are no doctors. There are no nurses. There are no medicines. There are not even gauze and lint to tie up a wound. Government hospitals anybody?

Now we have a whole cream of new, clean private hospitals. Is it not true that one of the clean private hospitals stitched a piece of textile into the backbone of the Chief Secretary as if they were textile people? In how many so-called private hospitals do you get anything which is called treatment?

Where are those servants of the people? They used to speak of ICS. It was not Indian. It was not civil and certainly was not a service. It was replaced by the service called the Indian Administrative Service. Most IAS people have learnt to say, 'I Am Sorry' because that is what the initials stand for.

Do you know the meaning of the word bureaucrat? The *Oxford Dictionary* gives the meaning as "those who follow rules." I wish there were more real bureaucrats in this country, and not the bogus surrogate bureaucrats who are doing Bharatnatyam, Kuchipudi, Manipuri and Oddissi rather than follow the rules.

Is it true or not that the quality of life in this country has reached an appalling level of degradation? When people with pride come and say he is an American, he is from Canada, he is from Australia, you say, "I am sorry, I am an Indian". What has converted you into this? How many of us sit down to think why we have reached this tragic state? Who is responsible for this mess?

The core of this mess is corruption — corruption of thought, corruption of deed, corruption of cash.

Tell me one thing in India which is not corrupt. It was during the French Revolution that Robespierre was described as the sea-green incorruptible. And he ended up at the gallows. Do you want me to analyse, dissent and vivisect corruption? Where did corruption come from? Corruption came because industry was pleased by all kinds of permits and licences. When Rajaji told you that "you are converting my country into a permit licence raj," you threw him out of the Governor-General's office, made him Home Minister and subsequently sent him as Chief Minister of Madras when the chair became too hot for anybody else to sit on. You will ask: "Are you a Rajaji worshipper?" I worship nothing because I am an iconoclast of the highest order. I have only one thing to worship. That is this beautiful daughter, this beautiful sister, this beautiful mother. "Which lady am I referring to? I have not seen any such person who is worthy of all this respect." I speak of the daughter called *Bharatmata*.

To me this woman of such fantastic variety can never be ruled by anything but democracy. Because if there are two Indians there are three opinions. I learnt my democracy long ago. The fundamental of this democracy is the right to disagree and not the right to agree. That is democracy, and I practised democracy long before the Greeks. In Athens they had got down to the plains, and decided that they will rule themselves by the rule of the people — *demos crasos*.

And we have to preserve this democracy. I want to tell you at the end of the day, please get up and fight. Please wake up. How shall we fight? We shall fight them in the streets. We shall fight them in the beaches. We shall fight them on the sands. But, do not use any violence because that day your movement will die. In every little thing that you do, fight that which is unjust. Don't start any all-India anti-corruption movement. It will die in two-and-a-half days. The treasurer will collect the money and run away with the cash. The secretary will run away with the stenographer if she has vague beauty. Do you want an all-India *brashtachar samiti*? There are a thousand of them. They are full of *brashtachars* themselves. In little places, make little cells, of not more than, say, five people. Never increase them beyond ten. When you become ten, make two cells because all healthy cells break. Only cancerous cells grow indefinitely and produce cancer. If five of you get together and get the poor fellow his ration card, a poor girl her marksheet, or somebody else whom justice has been prevented from reaching, reach that person to justice. "What do you promise us if this happens?" I promise you blood, sweat, toil and tears.

If I have made you poignant, if I have made you agonised, if I have made you distressed, I owe you no apology. My purpose is to wake you up. Would you like to continue to sleep in the waking posture? That is left to you. *Amen*.

Index

Abortion, 39, 74
Accountability, 27, 34
  disappearance of, 27
Achooth or Harijan, 19
Adi-Shankara's treatises *Shad Bhava Manasa Jata*, 21
Additional Election Commissioners, 51
Advani, Lal Krishna, 29
Agricultural production, 78
Aircrafts, devlopment in, 82
Aiyer, Alladi Krishnaswami, 18
All-India *brashtachar samiti*, 151
AICC Bombay session, 42
AIDMK, 24
AK-47, 27, 86
Alexander the Great, 87-88
Ambedkar, Bhimrao Ramji, 18, 19
Assam, 22, 31, 105

Assam Gana Parishad, 24
Attorney-General of India, 31, 68, 110
Azad, Abdul Kalam, 18, 19, 144

Basu, Jyoti, 31, 128
Bhagat, H.K.L., 122
Bhagwad Gita, 75, 141
BJP, 24
Bible, 36, 67, 94, 109
Bihar, 31, 105
Bihar constituency
  example of counting of votes in, 59-60
Biochemistry, achievement in, 145
Bioengineering
  achievement in, 145
Birth rate, 20, 78-79

Bodoland, 22
Bombay, 22
Booth-capturing, 20, 91, 127
Brain drain, 83
Buddhism, 96
Bureaucrat, meaning of, 149
   see also civil service

Caste and subcaste
   division of, 34, 70
CBI, 25
Cellular Jail, 144
Central Asia, 17, 78
Central Institute of Indian Languages,
   Hyderabad, 96
Central Reserve Police Force, 31
Chakma refugee issue, 133
Chandragupta Maurya, 87-88
Chandrasekhar, 36
Cherrapunji, annual rainfall at, 77
Chief Election Commissioner, 31, 46,
   48, 52, 58, 62, 90, 117-118,
   127, 128
Children of school-going age, number
   of, 83
Chowdhry, Renuka, 59
Christianity, 96, 139
Churchill, 47
Citizens' Consensus for Democracy or
   National Consensus, 131
City Police Act, 67
Civil disobedience, 88
Civil Service, 17, 24, 25, 35, 40,
   45-46, 72, 104-105, 123, 134,
   149
Clive, Lord Robert, 143
Coalfields, 10
Code of Conduct, 30
   see also Model Code of Conduct
Collectors of Customs, appointment
   of, 69
Commissioners, extra, 63
Commissioners of Income-Tax
   appointment of, 69
Commonwealth, 81
Computers, achievement in, 82
Concentration of wealth, 16

Concept of rule by consent, 89
Congress, 24
Constituencies, electoral, 89-90
Constituent Assembly, 52
Constitution, 9, 19, 48, 51, 60, 61,
   62, 64, 90, 99, 101, 102, 117,
   146, 166
Constitutional amendments, 102
Corruption or *brashtachar*, 12, 34,
   39, 40, 41, 47, 57, 72, 105, 108,
   111, 124, 133, 148-151
Cotton export, 145
Country-made guns, use of, 55, 86
CPI, 24
CPM, 24
Criminalisation of politics, 57, 111,
   UP Assembly MLAs' role in, 58-59,
   103
Culture, ancient and modern
   compared, 92

Dandi, 144
Death rate, 20, 78
Defection, 26, 102
Delhi election, 121-122, 124
Delimitation Commission, 54
Democracy
   meaning of, 91
   pillars of, 101, 105, 130
   principles of, 18-20
   protection of, 47-48, 150-151
Deshmukh, Chintaman, 104
Devanesan, Dr Chandran, memory
   of, 141-143, 146
Dhanoa, S.S., 61
Dharma, meaning of, 16
Dhoomketu, meaning of, 73
Director-General of Elections, 48
DMK, 24
Drinking water, 19-20, 115
Dyer, General, 144

East India Company, 87
Education, 12-13, 19-20, 39, 100,
   137, 146-147
   and leakage of question papers, 40,
   146

copying system in, 39
defects in, 147-148
elementary, 146
improvement in, 145-146
lack of, 83
tution system in , 40
valuation system in, 40
Elections, 22, 24, 116-119
corruption in, 27, 57, 108-109
criminality in, 57
defects in, 26-27, 28-31, 120-122, 155-156
information and disinformation during, 26
liquor role in, 27
malpractices in, 91
manipulative tactics of privileged professionals in, 12
money power role in, 27, 47
policemen force strength during, 90
suggestions for the improvement of, 31-32
Election account expenses, 46-47, 56-57, 125-126
Election booths, Bihar example, 22-23
Election Commission, 24-25, 30-32, 46, 52, 55, 56, 59, 61-62, 67, 68, 70, 74, 118-121, 134
staff strength of, 117
Election Commissioners, 118-119
Election expenditure limit, 56, 58, 69-70, 124-125
Election laws, need for change in, 28
Election rigging, 29-30, 91, 120-121, 127
Election symbols, 90
Election violence, 30
and death statistics in 1991 and 1993, 104
Elections in universities, 45
Electoral reforms, 111-112, 119-120, 124-125
Electoral rolls
Bangladeshis in, 90

mistakes in, 29
see also voters' lists
Employment, 19, 20
English language, 88
Environment, degradation of, 83-84, 106
Ethiopia, 17
Evaluation system, 38
Expenditure observers, 69

Fabian socialism, 81
Famine in Bengal, death statistics during, 81
Food, self-sufficiency and exporters, 10
Foodgrain
India as exporter of, 81
production, 81, 106
Freedom, erosion of, 17-18

Gandhi, Mahatma, 15, 16, 17, 19, 35, 88, 116, 144
Gandhi, Rajiv, 36, 42, 51
Gandhi, Sanjay, 115
Golden Jubilee of the Quit India Movement, 115
Government planes, misuse of, 31
Green Revolution, 10
Gresham's law of currency, 92
Gross national income, 20
Growth rate, 79
Gurukula, 146

Hazlitt, on education, 12
Health, 19-20, 39, 148-149
and malaria, 20, 78
and mosquitoes, 148
and plague, 148
and small-pox, 20, 148
and tuberculosis, 78
and typhoid, 20
Heisenberg principle, 74
Hinduism, 85-87, 96-97, 129, 139
Hindutwa, meaning of, 38
Home Secretary, 32
Hospitals, conditions of, 149
Housing, 20

Identity cards, 31, 65, 111-112
Impersonation cases, 53-54
Indian Administrative Service, 24, 38
    motto of, 38
    see also Civil Service
Indian Civil Procedure Code, 88
Indian Criminal Procedure Code, 88
Indian Institute of Technology, 83,
    114
Indian National Congress, Lahore
    session of, 81
Indian Penal Code, 69, 88
Industrial sector, achievement of, 16,
    145
Infant mortality, 79-80
Islam, 96, 139

Jainism, 96, 139
Jallianwala Bagh massacre, 144
Janata Cloth Scheme sari, 68-69
Janata Dal, 24
Jayalalitha, 128
Jews, 96
Jharkhand, 22
Journalists, limited contribution of,
    105
Judicial service, 17
Judiciary, 130
    collapse of, 40

Karkaria, Bachi, 33
Kashmir, 22, 105,
    author's report on, 34
Kerala, 21-22, 80, 115
Kerala elections, Air India hoarding
    during, 108
Khanna, Rajesh, 29, 121
Khayyam, Omar, 73
Khurana, Hargovind, 43
Krishnamurthy, Ghali Venkatagopala,
    63
Kurien, Dr., 106

Languages, 70, 87, 96
Law Department, 25

Law of occasional conformity (Britain),
    30
Leadership, 18-19
Life expectancy, 107
Literacy
    female, 21, 80, 107, 115
    in Kerala, 21-22, 80, 107
Liquor, role in elections of, 27
List system in Germany, 46
Lok Sabha, 64, 103, 104
Lucknow Lawyers' Forum, 50, 72, 74

Madras Christian College, 140
Manifesto, 132
Manipulation, tactics of, 28
Manipur, 22
MARG poll survey, 101
Milk production, 106, 145
Model Code of Conduct, 51-52, 60-
    61, 65-75, 120
Money allocation, misuse of, 20
Money power, 34, 47
Moral character, 35
Moral corruption, 25

Nagaland, 22, 105
Namibia, 17
Narmada river, 49
National Authorised Representative,
    121
National income, 20
National Literacy Mission, 115
National Parties, 24
Naxalites or PWG, 22, 47, 105
Nehru, Jawaharlal, 16-17, 19, 35,
    46, 81, 88, 131, 143, 144
Nehru, Motilal, 19
New Delhi constituency, 121
Noakhali, 15
Nutan Assam Gana Parishad, 124
Nutrition, 19, 20

Pakistan, US role in arming of, 80
Palghat, 76
Panchayat samiti, 27
Panchayati Raj, 27, 46

Panchayati Raj Constitution Amendment Bill, 61
Panchayati Raj Movement, 46
Pant, Govind Ballabh, 144
Parliament, 103, 118, 127, 128
Parliamentary elections
  candidates during, 36
  seats for, 36
Parsis, 96
Patel, Sardar, 19, 35, 103, 144
Per capita availability of land, 82
Per capita availability of laws, 101
Personal integrity, 19
Personality cult, creation of, 26
Physical security, absence of, 30
Pilate, Pontius, 27
Planned development, 81
Planning Commission, 83, 107
PL-480 wheat, 81
Policemen's force, 32, 90
Political parties, dirty role of, 55
Polling booths, 28
  defects in, 120
Polling officer (s), 29
Population, 53, 78, 115-116, 142-145
  Muslim, 84-85
Population control, cases of international success in, 79
Power-brokers, Rajiv Gandhi and, 42
Prasad, Dr. Rajendra, 18
President (of India), 51, 102, 118
President's rule, 119
Prime Minister, 61, 65, 109, 111
Privileged professionals, categories of, 12
Public awareness, significance of, 12
Pune, 16, 26
  as an industrial city, 16
Punjab, 22, 105
Punjab elections, postponement of, 109-110, 128

Quality of life, 19-22

Races, kinds of, 87
Railways, criticism of, 40-41
Rajagopalachari, C., 18, 145, 150
Rajya Sabha, 64, 102-103, 118-119
Rama Rao, N.T., 59
Rape case
  in Arabian deserts, 12
  in India, 12-13
RDX, 27
Recognized State parties, 24
Reddy, Vijay Bhaskar, 128
Registered and unregistered parties, 24
Religion, in India, 96, 129
Representation of the People Act, 56, 60, 64, 70, 103, 118
Republican Party, 24
Rice exports, 145
Rockets, development in, 82, 145
Rule of law, 11, 26

Sahay, Subodh Kant, 110
Saikia, 128
Sanskrit, 93
Sapru, Tej Bahadur, 18
Satellites, 82, 145
Saving rate, 80
Science and technology, corruption in, 41
Seshan, T.N.
  accusation against, 35-36
  and Laloo Yadav, 31
  as Alsatian, 90
  as environment secretary, 25
  as insane lunatic, 58
  as *Khalnayak,* 58, 72, 90
  as mad bull, 90
  as member of the ONGC, 29
  birth of, 76
  Civil Service career of, 76-77, 82, 123-124, 148
  education of, 76
  family background of, 76
  impeachment motion against, 126
  Jyoti Basu calling a mad dog, 31
  meeting with Rajiv Gandhi, 76

names given to, 31, 58, 90
report on Kashmir of, 34
Shakhder, 57, 60
Shankaranand, 68
Sharma, Naval Kishore, 122
Shastri, Lal Bahadur, 41
Shastri, Peri, 56, 60, 61
Sikhism, 96, 134
Singh, Bhagat, 144
Singh, Kaka Joginder, *urf Dharti Pakad*, 33
Singh, Manmohan, 103, 125-126
Sinha, Shatrughan, 29, 121
Slum Clearance Board, 145
Slums, 99, 115, 145
Socialism and planned development, 81
Somalia, 17
Sri Krishna, 35
Sri Rama, 35, 48
State Election Commissions, 61
State parties, 24
Statute Book, 54
Steel plants, 82
Steel production in India, 82
Supreme Court, 61, 63, 65, 66, 68, 69, 100, 101, 110, 119

Tagore, Rabindranath, 43, 75
Tamil Nadu elections, 110
Tatas, 82
Teacher-pupil ratio, 83
Techno-economic power, 11
Telephones, 17
percentage of successful calls, 40
Telephone Department, 40
Television channels, 16-17
Textile mills, 10, 81-82

Thomas, St., 93
Tilak, Bal Gangadhar, 26
Tiruchirapalli constituency, 29
Tripura election, example of IG and DIG of Police in collusion with politicians, 109
Trivedi, 57, 60

Unemployment statistics, 83
United Nations, 143
United States, 143
University Grants Commission, 146
UP Assembly, number of criminal MLAs in, 58-59, 103

Values, fragmentation of, 34-35
Vice-Chancellor (s), 100
Voters, number of, 89
Voters' lists or electoral lists, 29, 53, 90, 111
and Assam foreigners' issue, 128
defects in, 91, 120
statistics of, 116
Voting population, 90

Walpole, Horace, 30
Weapons, role of, 22, 27, 86
Weather variations, 84
West Bengal, 31
Wheat exports, 145
Women's education, neglect of, 113
Women voters, denial of voting rights to, 55
World Bank/IMF, 88

Yadav, Laloo, 128

Zila Parishads, 27